SO-AAC-661

CREATION

of the

MODERN MIDDLE EAST

Syria

CREATION

of the

MODERN MIDDLE EAST

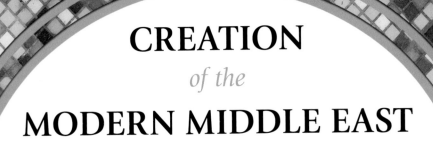

CREATION
of the
MODERN MIDDLE EAST

Syria

Second Edition

Jack Morrison | Additional text: Adam Woog

Series Editor: Arthur Goldschmidt Jr.

CHELSEA HOUSE
PUBLISHERS
An imprint of Infobase Publishing

Syria, Second Edition
Copyright ©2009 by Infobase Publishing

Chelsea House
An imprint of Infobase Publishing
132 West 31st Street
New York NY 10001

Library of Congress Cataloging-in-Publication Data
Morrison, John, 1929-
    Syria / Jack Morrison; with additional text by Adam Woog. — 2nd ed.
      p. cm. — (Creation of the modern Middle East)
    Includes bibliographical references and index.
    ISBN 978-1-60413-019-5 (hardcover)
    1. Syria—Juvenile literature. I. Woog, Adam, 1953- II. Title. III. Series.
    DS93.M58 2008
    956.91—dc22 2008012412

Chelsea House books are available at special discounts when purchased in bulk quantities for businesses, associations, institutions, or sales promotions. Please call our Special Sales Department in New York at (212) 967-8800 or (800) 322-8755.

You can find Chelsea House on the World Wide Web at
http://www.chelseahouse.com

Series design by Annie O'Donnell
Cover design by Jooyoung An

Printed in the United States of America

Bang FOF 10 9 8 7 6 5 4 3 2 1

This book is printed on acid-free paper.

Contents

After the Lion

Bashar al-Assad was too young to be president. The Syrian constitution said the president had to be 40 years old, and Bashar was only 34. Since his father, Hafez al-Assad, the man who had ruled Syria with an iron hand for 30 years, had chosen him as his successor, the constitution was quickly changed. Hafez al-Assad died on June 10, 2000, while talking on the telephone to the president of Lebanon. Some observers saw symbolism in the way he died—a conversation unfinished, as he had left unfinished not only his part in peace negotiations with Israel, with whom Syria was still technically at war, but the process of bringing his troubled and underdeveloped country into the twenty-first century. The question on everybody's mind that desperate June was whether Bashar, the mild-mannered eye doctor and computer whiz with no military or government background to speak of, could carry on the legacy of the "Lion of Damascus" (*Assad* means "lion" in Arabic) while at the same time taking at least some steps in the direction of modernization of a country generally viewed as a "backwater" of the Middle East. In a *New York Times* article, Thomas L. Friedman described Syria at the time of Hafez's death as "the last country in the Middle East to introduce fax machines and the Internet, a country with a crumbling industrial base, a corrupt, 19th-century banking system, an utterly backward educational system, and not a single world-class export of any product or service"—a harsh indictment of the 30-year rule of Hafez al-Assad.

In addition, the country had long been on the United States' list of countries that support terrorism. Terrorist training camps

Hafez al-Assad was president of the Syrian Arab Republic for three decades (1971–2000) and was one of the Middle East's longest serving leaders. Known as "The Lion," he is credited with bringing much-needed political stability to a country that experienced many difficult times after claiming independence from France in 1946.

had operated within Syria for many years, and their graduates went forth bent on the destruction of Israel and Israel's supporters. Although there was no evidence to link Syria with the September 11, 2001, attacks on New York City's World Trade Center and the Pentagon in Washington, D.C., the United States viewed any nation with links to terrorism as a possible threat. It was not good policy to be on bad terms with the world's only remaining superpower.

Hafez al-Assad was 69 and afflicted with a variety of serious ailments when he died. Knowing death was near, he began to groom Bashar as his successor. It was well known that Assad would have preferred his eldest son, Basil, a dashing military officer, to rule after his death, but Basil had been killed in a car crash in 1994.

So, Bashar was brought home from England, where he had been practicing ophthalmology, to begin training as the new leader of a land that had been trampled over and mauled for 4,000 years by most of the mighty empires of Earth, where corruption and inefficiency were rampant, and where many powerful men were looking askance at this young man and wondering if he was up to the job.

During Bashar's "training," his father gave him diplomatic tasks to perform, and he was pushed onto the public stage as much as possible so that he would not be a total unknown when his father died. In addition, father and son purged the administration of those who objected to the planned succession.

LEGACY OF HAFEZ AL-ASSAD

Bashar followed in the footsteps of a man whose major accomplishment in three decades had been staying in power. Hafez al-Assad was not very good at much more than survival. As a military leader, he lost all the battles he fought with Israel. As a man of peace, he was too stubborn to make the concessions necessary to reach agreements among governments, even though he had committed himself to seeking peace. At the time of his death, a deal with Israel seemed possible to some.

Hafez al-Assad knew how to keep a firm grip on power. He was ruthless in crushing his enemies and stifling dissent. He took control of a country that had endured 21 coups in as many years. Before Assad, government officials could barely get comfortable in their chairs before they were kicked out in

People throughout the world felt a great sense of loss when Hafez al-Assad died in June 2000. Foreign dignitaries such as French President Jacques Chirac and U.S. Secretary of State Madeleine Albright attended the funeral that was held in the Na'isa mosque, named after the Syrian president's mother. Here, a Syrian army officer watches as mourners parade past a mosque in the northern town of Qardaha.

favor of another equally incompetent group of leaders, who were shortly sent on their way as well. The coups may have been bloodless, but they kept this ancient country in a constant state of turmoil.

Hafez al-Assad ended this revolving-door style of government and brought stability and a sense of dignity to the Syrian people despite the harsh economic conditions under which many of them still lived.

When Assad's death was announced, the people crowded the streets of the capital city of Damascus and other Syrian cities and sent up an anguished chorus of regret. People cut themselves with knives, an expression of mourning. One woman rushed with the crowd to Assad's residence, beat her chest, and cried, "Say that he is not dead!"

An announcer on Damascus radio addressed the dead leader, saying, "Your soul is gone, but you are still with us."

Shops were shuttered, and the only business being done was by vendors selling long strips of black mourning cloth for banners and flags.

"It is like losing somebody very close," a 22-year-old laborer said of Hafez al-Assad. "I was one of his sons. The first thing I saw when I was born was President Assad." Would such warm sentiments be easily transferred to the new president? Only time would tell.

Meanwhile, Bashar's father's funeral brought heads of state or their representatives flocking to Damascus. In many Arab countries, flags flew at half-mast and official periods of mourning were declared. Even North Korea called a weeklong period of mourning.

The United States Secretary of State, Madeleine Albright, bowed her head briefly over Assad's casket. Palestinian leader Yasir Arafat, long a bitter enemy of Assad, saluted, then kissed Bashar and clung to his hand for several minutes of conversation.

Madeleine Albright returned from their meeting with a pledge from Bashar to follow in his father's footsteps: He agreed to continue the crucial peace talks with Israel. His father had agreed at a multilateral peace conference in Madrid in 1991 to consider peace negotiations with Israel. Since he had stubbornly clung to his demand that the Golan Heights, lost to the Israelis in the Six-Day War of 1967, be returned to Syria, little progress had been made. The Israeli government was adamant about retaining control of this region.

An article in the June 19, 2000, issue of *Newsweek* suggested that Assad had held out for one demand too many: "The main obstacle in Israeli-Syrian peace talks is but a few hundred disputed yards on the Sea of Galilee at the foot of the Golan Heights."

Former Israeli Prime Minister Shimon Peres commented, "Assad was always short a finger or two in reaching out to touch peace."

Because of such obstinacy, there were no expressions of mourning for Assad in Israel. A newspaper columnist wrote, "We Israelis have no reason to shed any tears over the death of Hafez al-Assad. It's a waste of water."

Such an attitude underlined the continuing hostility between the two countries that promised to make the struggle for a peace agreement a long, hard road, despite the arrival of a new man with, hopefully, new ideas on how to cope with the oldest and most intractable problem in the Middle East, and, by extension, the world.

A NEW LEADER

After his funeral, Hafez al-Assad was laid to rest in his hometown, the tiny mountain village of Qardaha, 125 miles northwest of Damascus. Thousands of people milled around the mosque Assad had built to honor his mother. Soldiers struggled to keep mourners from pushing forward to kiss the flag-draped coffin so that prayers for the dead could begin. He was entombed next to his son Basil in a grand mausoleum on a hill overlooking the town.

Then, after the customary three days of mourning, Bashar al-Assad emerged to take the reins of a country whose problems would stagger, and had staggered, men of greater age and experience in the complex and confounding politics of the Middle East.

Photographs of Bashar al-Assad in military fatigues were plastered on walls, an indication of his desire for vital military support and his desire to assume the mantle of his late father. Although he had little military experience, he held the rank of colonel. On ascending to the presidency, he was promoted to lieutenant general and became commander in chief of the military.

The mourners in the streets voiced their support for the new leader by chanting, "Bashar, we are with you!" Many of the young demonstrators had never known another regime except Hafez al-Assad's. They greeted the ascendancy of another Assad as the natural order of things.

On March 5, 2002, Syria announced its support of a peace plan proposed by Crown Prince Abdullah of Saudi Arabia. The proposal promised peace for Israel and its neighbors if Israel would give back the territory it took from the Arabs in the 1967 war, including the Golan Heights. Bashar al-Assad met with Abdullah to discuss the plan, then announced the Syrian position; however, there did not seem to be any likelihood that the Israelis would accept the plan, so the position was meaningless.

An earlier indication that Bashar was still strongly under the influence of the hardliners in his government came when Syria used its first public appearance after its election to membership on the United Nations Security Council on January 19, 2002, to unleash a withering criticism of Israel. At the time, Israel was trying to put down a Palestinian rebellion in Gaza and the West Bank, territories controlled by Israel since their capture in the June 1967 war.

Syria's UN representative, Fayssal Mekdad, assailed the destruction of Palestinian homes in Gaza by Israeli troops seeking to root out terrorists, and likened the action to the terrorist attacks on America. Coming as it did shortly after the 9/11 attacks in the United States, this connection seemed outrageous to U.S. diplomats, and they denounced it harshly.

Mekdad also defended anti-Israeli militants, criticized America's support of Israel, and urged the council to shift the focus of its counterterrorism campaign to Israel. It appeared to many that Syria continued to be preoccupied with opposing Israel to the exclusion of other important considerations, and that it intended to try to stir up the rest of the world against the Israelis.

What did this tell the world about the policies of the new regime in Syria? Was it going to foster the same foreign policy as before? It seemed that young Bashar was afraid that if he did not appease the hard-liners, he might become a victim of another of those ceaseless coups that had plagued the country before his father took over.

He was certainly aware that despite the support of the people in the streets, and, for the moment at least, the backing of the military, there were those waiting in the wings, watching him carefully, and formulating their plans. Among them were not only his father's old enemies, but members of his own family, such as his angry uncle Rifaat, who had vowed to return from the exile into which his brother Hafez had sent him in order to retain power himself. Even Bashar's younger brother Maher, who had made his career in the military, was waiting in the wings with his own ambitions and hoping to take charge.

How young Bashar would navigate the future was of vital interest not only to Syria and the Middle East, but to the world, since reverberations from conflicts in that dangerous region have always had, and will continue to have, an international impact.

2

Land of Abraham

Syria is a land of Bible stories. The very stones speak of history and legend. Muslims believe Damascus was the original Garden of Eden—that God fashioned Adam from the clay of the Barada River. It is where many believe the long centuries of man's fall from grace began when Adam and Eve were expelled from paradise after tasting the forbidden fruit of the Tree of Knowledge. It is also where Cain is supposed to have killed Abel in the world's first murder and hidden the corpse in a grotto. Abel's supposed tomb is outside Damascus, where a crimson streak of rock is said to be his blood spilling over the ground.

Syria's significance in religious history continues in the story of St. Paul. Paul was a Jew, a Pharisee, and a Roman citizen, who, while on his way to Damascus from Jerusalem to fight the Christians, was knocked off his horse and blinded by a celestial light. He then became a convert to Christianity. A shrine was built six miles south of Damascus to mark the traditional place of his conversion. Here also Abraham had been born and had built an altar to his God. Moses and Lot and Job, figures from the Old Testament, had prayed there. King David had conquered here, as had Alexander the Great centuries later. The soldiers of many mighty empires had marched over this ancient ground. All of them left their mark on the land and the people, who seemed forever to be altering their culture and religion to accommodate the new rulers.

Greater Syria once included what are now the countries of Israel, Jordan, and Lebanon, as well as parts of Turkey. In 1918, following World War I, the region was carved up by the British. Syria now is a nation of 71,498 square miles, bordered by Iraq,

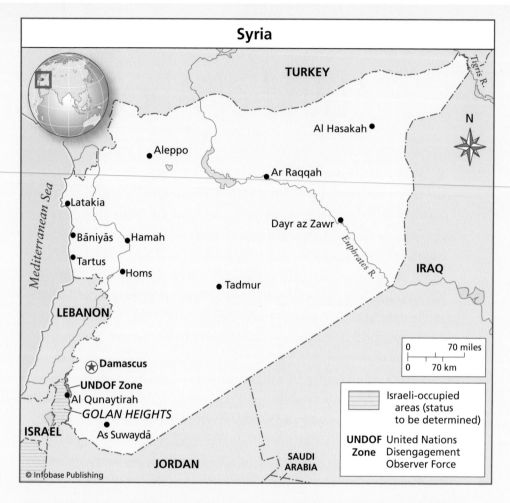

Syria

TURKEY

Al Hasakah

Aleppo

Ar Raqqah

Mediterranean Sea

Latakia

Dayr az Zawr

Bāniyās   Hamah

Tartus

Euphrates R.

IRAQ

Homs

Tadmur

LEBANON

Tigris R.

N

Damascus

UNDOF Zone

Al Qunaytirah

GOLAN HEIGHTS

As Suwaydā

ISRAEL

JORDAN

SAUDI
ARABIA

0	70 miles
0	70 km

Israeli-occupied
areas (status
to be determined)

UNDOF United Nations
Zone Disengagement
Observer Force

© Infobase Publishing

Although Syria is a relatively small country, its borders once stretched into Israel, Jordan, and Lebanon, but shrank after the British redrew the lines in the region. Reluctant to lose more land to other countries, Syria has demanded territories lost to Israel during the Six-Day War be returned to Syrian control.

Jordan, Israel, and Turkey, with a short coastline on the Mediterranean Sea. Many Syrians still resent the loss of so many lands and peoples formerly associated with their country.

Syria's people are mostly Arabs, and the major religion is Islam, although there are other ethnic and religious minorities, including

Christians. People who follow the religion of Islam (*Islam* is Arabic for "submission") are called Muslims (Arabic for "one who submits [to God]"). Among the most prominent Islamic sects in Syria are the Alawis (or Alawites) and the Druze. Both of these sects have played important roles in the country's modern history.

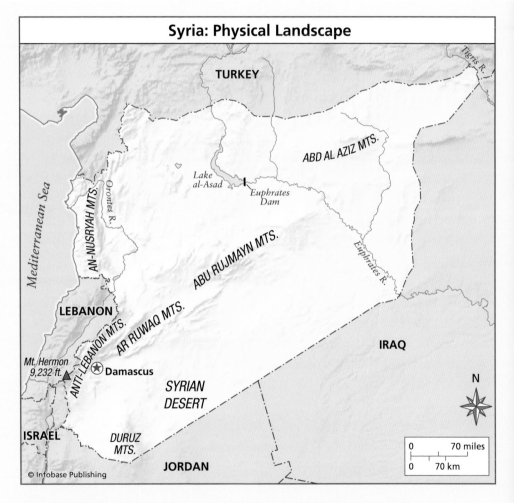

Syria: Physical Landscape

With a Mediterranean coastline and several rivers and tributaries, Syria has managed to develop an agricultural industry while also encouraging trade and tourism. Meanwhile, the mountains located in the southwestern region of the country provide protection from Israel and Lebanon.

For centuries, camel caravans traveled back and forth across Syria, carrying goods between Asia and Mediterranean ports. As a result, Syrian cities like Damascus and Aleppo became major world trade centers as early as 2000 B.C.

The country is on the western end of the Fertile Crescent, so called because of its well-watered, arable farmland. Thus, agriculture was a major industry in Syria for centuries, and still is an important part of the economy today. About half its population (a total of some 18.6 million) lives in rural areas. Some of these are Bedouins, nomads who live in tents and travel over the countryside with their livestock.

More than 3 million people live in Damascus, one of the world's most ancient cities. It is so old that no one really knows when it was first established. One legend holds that it was founded by Uz, great-grandson of Noah. Another says that it was begun by Demschak, a slave of Abraham. Those legendary tales only emphasize the mystery of the city's origins.

The Roman emperor Julian (A.D. 361–363) described it as "the city which in very truth belongs to Zeus and is the eye of the whole east—sacred and most mighty Damascus."

Yet, from the seventh century on, Damascus belonged to Muslims. After centuries of being under the control of Akkadians, Canaanites, Aramaeans, Assyrians, Babylonians, Persians, Greeks, Seleucids, Romans, and Byzantines, Syria was conquered in A.D. 636 by Muslim armies from the Arabian Peninsula.

PROPHET MUHAMMAD

One night early in A.D. 632, the Prophet Muhammad, founder of the Muslim community, called a servant to tell him he had received a summons from the dead in the graveyards of Medina, a city in what is now Saudi Arabia, to pray for them. The two went out into the night to find the cemetery, and, after his prayers, Muhammad predicted that he would soon die. At the time, Muhammad's Muslim armies were massed at the border of Syria, then ruled by the Christian Byzantine Empire, and were about to invade, but Muhammad became ill soon after his visit to the cemetery, and they decided to wait. Muhammad collapsed while leading Friday prayers, but he managed to raise himself up and tell his frightened people, "Has any prophet before me lived forever, that you thought I would never leave you? I return to him who sent me. My life has been good; so will be my death."

A few days later, he uttered his final words: "Oh, Allah, be it so! Henceforth among the glorious host of Paradise!" And so the main prophet of what would become one of the world's major religions died. After his death, his armies, led by his disciple Abu Ubayda, invaded Syria and captured Damascus.

Within 20 years of Muhammad's death, his followers, obeying the principle of *jihad*, or holy war, had established the first Islamic empire in the Fertile Crescent, conquering the Persians and Byzantines, and within 100 years Muslims had created an empire that stretched from northern Spain to India. They were stopped from invading France in the Battle of Tours in A.D. 732.

PEOPLE AND CULTURE

The Muslims created a flourishing civilization in Iraq, Persia (now Iran), North Africa, Spain, and Syria. Culture and arts flourished. They built many magnificent structures, like the Alhambra in Spain and the Taj Mahal in India. Under Caliph Uthman, who ruled the Islamic world after Muhammad's death, the Koran—the holy book of the Muslims (from an Arabic word meaning "recitation")—was put together from Muhammad's revelations.

Over the years, Muslims split into various sects. The two largest are the Sunni and the Shiite. Most Muslims, including most of those in Syria, are Sunnis. They believe that Muslim leadership after the death of Muhammad passed to caliphs elected from Muhammad's tribe, the Quraysh, which claimed descent from the Bible's Ishmael. The Shiites believe that leadership was restricted to descendants of Ali, Muhammad's son-in-law. These may seem like insignificant differences to outsiders, but the unequal balance of power between the Sunnis and the Shiites was crucially important.

Muslims of all sects believe in one God, called Allah. The belief in one God had been brought into Syria in the late 1200s B.C. by Hebrews. Although Arabs and Jews share the belief in one deity, in modern times they have been at odds over questions of power and land.

The Koran includes stories from the Judeo-Christian Bible, and Muslims honor many of the same prophets, including the Old Testament patriarchs and Jesus. They believe that Muhammad was the last of the prophets and that there will be no more.

HISTORY OF SYRIA

The most ruthless of the many invaders of the Middle East had to have been the Christian Crusaders. In a series of invasions meant to wrest the Holy Lands from the "heathen" Muslims, the Crusaders felt compelled by religious fervor to slaughter Muslim men, women, and children, and did so with ruthless abandon.

In 1099, the Crusaders took Jerusalem after a 40-day siege and proceeded to kill most of the Muslim population. They did not restrict their murderous onslaught to Muslims, however. They trapped a congregation of Jews in their synagogue, surrounded it, and burned it to the ground. They made sure every single Jew burned to death.

Similar depredations were carried out in Damascus, although the Crusaders never took that city. Abu Sa'ad al-Harawi, the *qyadii*, or senior judicial officer in Damascus, was so shaken by sights of murder and destruction that he shaved his head in mourning. When he arrived at the palace of the Caliph al-Mustazhir in Baghdad to tell his tale, he was shocked to find the ruler and members of his court taking their ease in luxurious surroundings: "How dare you slumber in the shade of complacent safety, leading lives as frivolous as garden flowers, while your brothers in Syria have no dwelling place save the saddles of camels and the bellies of vultures?" he demanded. "Never have

The Citadel of Aleppo dates back to at least the middle of the third millennium B.C. and was subsequently occupied by Greeks, Byzantines, Ayyubids, and Mamluks. In the thirteenth century it evolved into a palatial city that included shrines, palaces, military installations, and supporting elements like water cisterns and granaries. In 1986, it was declared a UNESCO World Heritage site, and today it is an important tourist attraction and the site of major archaeological digs.

the Muslims been so humiliated. Never have their lands been so savagely devastated."

It was not until 1187 that the Kurdish warrior Salah al-Din (also known as Saladin), sultan of Egypt, who had created a powerful kingdom out of Egypt and Syria, defeated the Crusaders at the Battle of Hattin. Even though there was a third and final Crusade in Syria, the Christian intruders never again spread their conquest so far.

The history of Syria was bloody for many centuries. Notable events included most of the land being taken by the Mongols in 1260 and then won back by the Mamluks of Egypt, a Muslim military caste. In 1401 came the part-Mongol, part-Turkish Muslim invader Timur (Tamerlane), who sacked and burned Damascus and Aleppo, setting back Syrian civilization and culture many decades.

Then arose the Turkish Ottoman Empire, which engulfed Syria in 1516, under the leadership of Sultan Selim I, and made Syria part of its vast empire. It held on until World War I, except for a brief intrusion by the Egyptians in the 1830s. (A combined force of British, Ottoman, and Austrian troops ousted the Egyptians in 1840, and the Ottomans took over again.)

The Ottomans made a big mistake at the outbreak of World War I by deciding to back Germany in the war, and it was this decision that led, after years of turmoil, discontent, and unwanted French rule, to the eventual independence of the state of Syria.

3

Lawrence of Arabia

Just five feet five-and-a-half inches tall, he was a little man. Still, he was as strong and tough as an Arabian saddle, and he had the endurance of a desert camel. In fact, it was said he could jump from a galloping camel while holding a heavy rifle and hop back on again in midstride. He was Thomas Edward Lawrence, best known as T.E. Lawrence and "Lawrence of Arabia." He was the man who led the Arabs in many of the crucial battles that brought an end to the mighty Ottoman Empire during World War I and the liberation of the Middle East from the Turks and their German allies. When he rode with his Arab forces into Damascus on October 1, 1918, to the wild acclaim of its citizens, it was the dramatic conclusion of a campaign that saw his desert forces, often battling against enormous odds, surge to a victory that would change the face of the Middle East forever.

The Ottoman Empire had ruled over the Arabs since 1516, but it was doomed by its fateful decision to align itself with the wrong side—Germany—in World War I. As a result, it was consigned to the dustbin of history, with all the other once-mighty empires that had ruled the Middle East over a span of 4,000 years.

What Lawrence, as a young English intelligence officer, brought to the Arabs in their fight against the Turks was British money and arms and the tactics of guerrilla warfare that enabled the Arabs to harass and confuse the Turkish and German forces. (Some of these tactics have been adopted by the fighters against the United States in Iraq.)

A man of amazing courage, Lawrence—garbed in the flowing robes and headpiece of the Arabs, a curved dagger in his

T.E. Lawrence, known throughout the world as Lawrence of Arabia, was a British soldier and adventurer famous for his role in helping the Arabs fight the Turks during World War I and for his vivid writings about the Middle East. He adopted many local customs and traditions, such as riding camels and wearing Arab clothing, and became disillusioned with his country's Middle East policies.

waistband, riding his favorite camel, Jedha—thundered into battle against artillery and machine-gun fire with reckless abandon. And he earned his Arabic nickname of *Emir Dinamit*, or Prince Dynamite, by blowing up railroad bridges to disrupt Turkish military transportation.

"For years we [Lawrence and his cohorts] lived anyhow with one another in the naked desert, under the indifferent heaven," he wrote in his classic book, *Seven Pillars of Wisdom*. "By day the hot sun fermented us; and we were dizzied by the beating wind. At night we were stained by dew, and shamed into pettiness by the innumerable silences of stars.

"We were a self-centered army without parade or gesture, devoted to freedom, the second of man's creeds, a purpose so ravenous that it devoured all our strength, a hope so transcendent that our earlier ambitions faded in its glare."

He was a romantic and a poet. His *Seven Pillars of Wisdom* begins with a poem, part of which reads, "I drew these tides of men into my hands and wrote my will across the sky in stars."

Still, the horrors of battle were always with him and haunted his days and dreams for the rest of his eccentric life.

"Blood was always on our hands; we were licensed to it," Lawrence wrote. "Wounding and killing seemed ephemeral pains, so very brief and sore was life with us. With the sorrow of living so great, the sorrow of punishment had to be pitiless. We lived for the day and died for it. When there was reason and desire to punish we wrote our lesson with gun or whip immediately in the sullen flesh of the sufferer, and the case was beyond appeal. The desert did not afford the refined slow penalties of courts and jails."

One night early in the campaign, he and his wartime companion and friend, Faisal, a future king of Syria and later Iraq, were dining with the fierce Arab fighter Auda ibu Tayi. Suddenly Auda leaped up with a cry of, "God forbid!"

He ran out of the tent, and soon the other diners heard a loud hammering. It was Auda pounding his false teeth to fragments on a stone.

"I had forgotten," he explained, "that Jemal Pasha (the Turkish commander in Syria who had hanged many Arab leaders) gave me these. I was eating my Lord Faisal's bread with Turkish teeth!" Fortunately, he had enough teeth left to finish the meal. Such was the ferocity of feeling against the hated Turks.

On October 1, 1918, Lawrence made a grand entry into Damascus, riding in a Rolls-Royce with Faisal, Auda, and an array of other remarkable heroes, in advance of General Edmund Allenby's Egyptian Expeditionary Force. The night before, the victors had been shocked when they heard explosions in the city. They feared that the retreating German troops had set it on fire. The next morning, Lawrence described the sight he saw: "Instead of ruins, the silent gardens stood blurred green with river mist, in whose setting shimmered the city, beautiful as ever, like a pearl in the morning sun."

Faisal was briefly the leader of a pan-Arab state based in Damascus. Hopes arose for the treasured ideal of Arab unity and independence, which Lawrence, Faisal, and many others had fought for. They believed they had British assurances of independence once the Ottomans were defeated.

Great Britain had promised to support an independent Arab state or a confederation of Arab states before the war as a way of getting the Arabs to join the Allies in subduing the Germans and Turks. (This had been agreed to in 1915 between the British and Faisal's father, Sharif Hussein.) The secret Sykes-Picot Agreement of May 16, 1916, later the basis for the postwar League of Nations mandates, granted Great Britain control of Iraq, Transjordan (later Jordan), and parts of Palestine (which was separated from Greater Syria), and the French oversight of Syria and Lebanon. The existence of the Sykes-Picot Agreement was kept secret from the Arabs by the Western powers but was revealed later, by the Russians, following the 1917 Bolshevik Revolution. (The Russian Bolsheviks, or Communists, wanted to discredit the Allies.)

Faisal had become king of Syria, but he was violently ousted by the French. (Faisal had refused to recognize the mandate that the French had been given over Syria by the League of Nations.) As compensation, the British installed him as king of Iraq, then called Mesopotamia. His brother Abdullah, originally slated to become king of Iraq, became king of Transjordan.

Lawrence was seriously disillusioned by Faisal's ouster by the French. The brief moment of Syrian independence had kindled his hopes that his Arab brethren might indeed attain freedom. But despite this setback, he still had hope, because of one man— Winston Churchill.

Churchill, who was named British colonial secretary in 1921, asked Lawrence to advise him on Middle Eastern policy. But it was difficult for many of the professional British soldiers to take this brash young man seriously. In one encounter at the Majestic Hotel in Paris, headquarters of the British delegation at a peace conference in 1919, a British general confronted him. Lawrence tried treating the officer with mild respect, but the officer must have detected a note he didn't like in Lawrence's demeanor.

"Don't dare to speak to me in that tone," the general huffed. "You're not a professional soldier."

"No," Lawrence said, "perhaps I'm not, but if you had a division and I had a division, I know which of us would be taken prisoner."

Lawrence's acerbic sense of humor might have eased the strains of battle and diplomacy, but it tended to alienate some of the pompous officers he had to deal with.

Once, on a raid, Lawrence was compelled to leave his medical officer behind. The British surgeon general demanded in a telegram to know how Lawrence planned to deal with his wounded without a medical officer.

His telegraphed reply: "Will shoot all cases too hurt to ride off."

DIVIDING THE MIDDLE EAST

Lawrence had been so discouraged in 1919 by what he viewed as treachery by Great Britain and France in failing to give the Arabs independence that he refused to accept medals the British government wanted to give him. Yet, in his role of adviser to Churchill, Lawrence felt strides were made that would bring both peace and eventual independence to the troubled region.

"I take to myself credit for some of Mr. Churchill's pacification of the Middle East, for while he was carrying it out he had the help of such knowledge and energy as I possess," he wrote in a letter to an author of a book about the revolt in the desert. "His was the imagination and courage to take a fresh departure and enough skill and knowledge of political procedure to put his political revolution into operation in the Middle East. . . . When it was in working order, in March 1922, I felt that I had gained every point I wanted."

The Arabs, he felt, "had their chance and it was up to them, if they were good enough, to make their own mistakes and profit by them."

Not everybody shared Lawrence's optimism for lasting peace for the region. Field Marshall Earl Wavell parodied the famous saying that World War I was a "war to end all wars" by commenting that the state of affairs after the war was a "peace to end all peace." Great Britain and France had carved up the Middle East without regard to the needs and desires of the Arab population. For example, the Kurds were originally promised their own homeland, but they ended up divided among Iraq, Iran, Syria, and Turkey, where they continue their struggle for independence to this day. Originally, the two Ottoman provinces of Basra and Baghdad comprised Iraq. Later Great Britain added the oil-bearing province of Mosul in the north. (Under Sykes-Picot, Mosul would have belonged to the French in Syria.) This action dashed the Kurds' hopes and angered the Sunni and Shiite Muslim sects.

Journalists Pierre Salinger and Erik Laurent commented, "Iraq was created by Churchill, who had the mad idea of joining two widely separated oil wells, Kirkuk and Mosul, by uniting three widely separated peoples: the Kurds, the Sunnis and the Shiites." Churchill liked to brag that he had created Transjordan with the stroke of a pen and then had time in the afternoon to paint a landscape.

Meanwhile, another situation was turning into early violence. In 1917, British Foreign Secretary Arthur Balfour sent a letter to Lord Rothschild, a leading British Zionist, pledging Great Britain's support for a national homeland for the Jewish people in Palestine. (Zionism was a movement begun in the nineteenth century that sought to achieve a Jewish homeland in Palestine.) Known as the Balfour Declaration, it led inevitably to clashes between the Jews and Arabs that continue into the twenty-first century.

While the Jewish "problem" was not paramount in T.E. Lawrence's association with Churchill and the peace process after World War I, it had a profound impact on the Middle East that emerged from the war.

One morning in 1921, when Churchill was touring the Middle East, he made a brief stop in Gaza, in Palestine, and was greeted by a cheering crowd. "Cheers for the Minister! Cheers for Great Britain!" the crowd chanted. What Churchill, who could not understand Arabic, did not hear were the even louder outcries: "Down with the Jews!" and "Cut their throats!"

Arab riots broke out throughout Palestine and in Jerusalem. In Haifa, police fired on a crowd, killing a 13-year-old Christian Arab boy and a Muslim Arab woman.

At a dinner with Emir Abdullah, future king of Jordan, Churchill said that while Jews would continue to be allowed to enter Palestine, "the rights of the existing non-Jewish population would be strictly preserved."

While Abdullah was optimistic, the rest of the Arab population was not. The Arabs petitioned Churchill to end Jewish immigration, at least until a Palestinian government could be established, but Churchill refused; he was bound by the Balfour Declaration. "It is manifestly right that the Jews, who are scattered all over the world, should have a national center and a national home where some of them may be reunited," he said. "And where else could that be but in this land of Palestine, with which for more than three thousand years they have been intimately and profoundly associated?"

While a Jewish minority had lived in Palestine for centuries and small-scale Jewish immigration was accepted, larger influxes were resisted by Arab Palestinians. Resistance grew firmer after the Balfour Declaration supported the establishment of a Jewish national home in Palestine, and hostilities punctuated the 1920s and 1930s. Here, an anti-Zionist demonstration is taking place in front of the U.S. consulate in Palestine on February 27, 1920.

To the Jews of Palestine, Churchill proclaimed that Zionism was a "great event in the world's destiny." The Jews, he said, would bring prosperity, "which would benefit all the inhabitants; no Arabs would be dispossessed."

Some of those statements seem extremely naive considering events that gradually unfolded over the next 80 years.

Meanwhile, T.E. Lawrence continued to hope for a unified Arab territory whose center would be located in Baghdad rather than Damascus, because Syria had become a less significant region than Iraq. He was right about that, but there was to be no Arab union. It remained an elusive dream that not many in the Middle East even bother to entertain anymore.

After his work with Churchill, Lawrence withdrew from public life, although publication of his *Seven Pillars of Wisdom* and its acclaim as a masterpiece brought him back into the public eye briefly.

In 1922, he enlisted in the British Royal Air Force as a private and adopted new names, first J.H. Ross and later T.E. Shaw. No one knew why he changed his name, except that he did not like acclaim and hid from the fame that other men would have treasured.

Lawrence never married and lived alone most of the time in an isolated cottage in Dorset. He died on May 19, 1935, after a motorcycle accident. He was 46.

4

A Taste of Freedom

In one of his videotaped harangues against the West after the September 11, 2001, terrorist attacks on the New York World Trade Center and the Pentagon in Washington, D.C., terrorist boss Osama bin Laden had a message for the world. He said that what the American people had suffered in the attacks was nothing compared to what the Arabs had been suffering for more than 80 years. His reference to 80 years took some people by surprise, since the usual Islamic complaint against the West refers to events going back at least 1,000 years. It sent some historians scrambling to find out what had happened "more than 80 years ago." Of course, bin Laden meant the October 1917 Balfour Declaration—an event seen by many Arabs as the source of eight decades of turmoil and despair.

Arabs had been harboring resentment over what they saw as multiple double-crosses by the West. Among these were the Hussein-McMahon Correspondence, which reportedly promised an independent and united Arab state under Hashemite rule in 1915; the secret Sykes-Picot Agreement, in which Great Britain and France agreed to divide up the Middle East; and the Balfour Declaration, with its promise of a Jewish homeland in Palestine.

At the time, there were 690,000 Arabs in Palestine, compared to 85,000 Jews. By 1948, Jews came to outnumber the Arabs, and they subsequently established their right to exist in three wars with their neighbors. Some 700,000 Palestinians went into exile, to the growing chagrin of their Middle Eastern neighbors, who had to take them in.

Perhaps bin Laden should not have been as resentful as most. His homeland, what is now Saudi Arabia, was left pretty much alone by the Allies after the war. The main problem for the Saudi monarchy was to conquer the Arabian Peninsula, including the Hijaz, which was ruled by Sharif Hussein up to 1924. Such problems were of their own making, not imposed by outside forces, as in Syria and the other Arab states. As T.E. Lawrence put it, the Arabs in Arabia were free to make their own mistakes and learn from them.

SYRIA UNDER FRENCH CONTROL, 1920–1946

In the rest of the Arab world, external interference was the rule. In response to the Sykes-Picot Agreement and the League of Nations mandate, French troops marched from Beirut to Damascus in 1920 to take over Syria. The Arabs put up a fight, but they were overwhelmed. It would not be the last time that French guns were turned on the Syrians before the final pullout of the French in 1946.

The brief period of Syrian self-government after World War I, when Faisal was king, had given nationalists in the country a taste of freedom, and many continued to fight for that freedom against the French. Among those touching off the revolts was Ibrahim Hannanu, who in 1919 incited a rebellion in an area controlled by France near the Turkish border. Although it and other resistance movements were brutally suppressed by the French, both Faisal and Hannanu have gone down in Syrian history as heroes of independence.

One important condition of the French mandate in Syria and Lebanon was that it was to be temporary, to allow for eventual independence. The French appeared to have lost sight of this specification. They ruled Syria with an iron hand; nearly every feature of Syrian life came under French control. Children were required to speak French and sing "La Marseillaise," France's national anthem. The franc became the currency of the economy, and currency management was in the hands of French bankers, who were more concerned with French shareholders and interests than with those of the Syrian people. Furthermore, to the Syrians and Lebanese, the franc was unstable compared to the pound sterling used in the British mandates.

Meanwhile, the Arab nationalist movement in Syria was led by educated, wealthy Muslims whose grievances against the French included suppression of newspapers, political activity, and civil rights. The French set out to weaken this movement by dividing the country into separate regions and giving support to religious minorities. Of particular concern was the separation of Lebanon, which came to be dominated by Maronite Christians, from Syria. Syria has never fully acquiesced in this separation. The two main parties of Syria were the People's Party, which favored reunification of the Fertile Crescent under Hashemite rule, and the National Bloc, which favored Egypt. Both were nationalistic and promoted civil liberties.

THE PEOPLE REBEL

Violence broke out in separate uprisings by Alawis, Druzes, and Bedouins, but these, like the other efforts at liberation, were put down by the French. A more serious rebellion by the Druzes occurred in 1925. The Druzes were an offshoot of Islam that controlled the Jabal Druze, a region in southern Syria. Their revolt against the French quickly spread throughout the country, igniting rebellions by other ethnic and religious groups in Aleppo and Damascus. After heavy fighting, the French ended the revolt by the systematic bombardment of Damascus, killing about 5,000 Syrians.

In 1928, the French allowed the formation of the National Bloc, composed of various nationalist groups centered in Damascus. It included leading members of large landowning families. The National Bloc wrote a constitution, which the French put into effect—after deleting all references to independence.

The Syrian nationalists wanted a treaty with France that would spell out French intentions toward the country. Great Britain and Iraq had signed such a treaty in 1922. A general strike in 1936 helped persuade the French, under Léon Blum's liberal-socialist government, to negotiate such a treaty, called the Syrian-French Treaty of Alliance, that year. The French parliament never ratified the treaty, but at that time the Syrians believed an important step had been taken for eventual self-rule.

Finally, with French approval, the first Syrian nationalist government came to power in 1936, with Hashim al-Atassi, one of the founders of the National Bloc, as president.

All this fell apart in 1939 when France agreed to hand over to Turkey the northern province of Alexandretta, later Hatay, a port on the Mediterranean with a large Turkish minority. Many Syrians blamed the Atassi government for the loss, and Atassi resigned. France again governed the unruly country. It looked like Syria's second serious attempt at self-government had failed.

Hitler's Germany was about to change everything. The Germans quickly conquered France in 1940 shortly after the outset of World War II and set up the Vichy government to run France and carry out Hitler's policies.

This meant that Syria was now governed by Vichy France. Still, Vichy's hold on Syria was a fragile one. British and Free French forces under General Charles de Gaulle, combined with the Transjordan Arab Legion, defeated the Vichy forces in both Syria and Lebanon. De Gaulle promised eventual independence for Syria, but the French Mandate remained in effect even under the Free French.

With the National Bloc now in control, Syrians elected a new parliament in 1943 and began taking over functions of the government, including those dealing with customs, social affairs, excise taxes, and other matters. The French retained control of social, cultural, and educational services, as well as of the peace-keeping force, called the Troupes Speciales du Levant. ("The

Residents of Damascus cheer as Free French troops ride on tanks through the city following the evacuation of Vichy forces. French general Charles de Gaulle and Free French troops refused to accept the surrender and collapse of France to the Axis forces during World War II and continued to fight against Germany. With British troops, they invaded and subdued Syria in 1941.

Levant" referred to Syria, Lebanon, and Palestine, although the French did not have troops in British-mandated Palestine.)

In July 1944, to the dismay of the French, the Soviet Union recognized Syria and Lebanon unconditionally as sovereign states. The United States followed in September, and British recognition followed a year later. These nations began pressuring France to get out of the region.

In January 1945, Syria belatedly entered World War II on the side of the Allies. It declared war on the Axis powers in February 1945, having formed a national army. (This was too late to see action, as the European theater of the war ended in May 1945.) In March, the country became a charter member of the United Nations. (Egypt and Syria were original members of the United Nations. In 1958, with the establishment of the United Arab Republic, Egypt and Syria would continue as a single member. In 1961, Syria would resume being an independent state and become a separate member in the United Nations.)

At the same time, Syria affirmed its allegiance to the idea of Arab unity by signing the pact of the League of Arab States. It has remained a member ever since, even though the Arab League failed to do much to promote Arab unity.

The European phase of World War II ended in May 1945, but the French were not finished with Syria, and even more blood would be spilled before they vacated the region for good.

In May 1945, there were violent demonstrations against the French occupation in Damascus and Aleppo. Once again the French bombed and fired on the ancient capital. Serious fighting broke out in Homs and Hamah as well. It was only after Winston Churchill, then the British prime minister, threatened to send in troops to restore order—a potentially humiliating move—that General de Gaulle ordered a cease-fire.

French control of Syria finally was grinding to a halt. In February 1946, the United Nations passed a resolution calling on France to evacuate the country. The French agreed, and by April 1946, all French troops were off Syrian soil. (April 17 is now celebrated as Evacuation Day, a national holiday in Syria.)

The celebration would be short-lived, as the effects of the Balfour Declaration soon would become apparent, dominating the attention of Syria as well as her Arab neighbors.

Under pressure from the Arabs, the British, although having issued the Balfour Declaration in 1917, had begun severely limiting immigration of Jews into Palestine. In May 1939, Great Britain had issued a white paper that came close to repudiating the Balfour Declaration. It placed severe limitations on Jewish immigration and land purchases and offered independence to a presumably Arab-dominated Palestine after ten years.

The British badly underestimated the determination of Jews worldwide, especially those from Europe. Europe was not only where the Nazis slaughtered six million Jews in the Holocaust, it was where Jews had been subjected to repeated pogroms (organized massacres of helpless people) and other outrages for centuries. The atrocities of the Holocaust took place after the British had issued the white paper, but it made clear the need for a Jewish national home or state.

PALESTINE IS CUT IN TWO

On November 29, 1947, the United Nations passed a historic resolution, opposed by every Arab member of the UN General Assembly. It partitioned Palestine into two independent states, one Jewish and one Arab. At midnight on May 14, 1948, the Jews proclaimed the State of Israel. These actions would change the face of the Middle East forever.

5

Birth of
a Nation

Five Arab nations—Syria, Lebanon, Iraq, Egypt, and Jordan—were invading the new country even as Moshe Sharett, foreign minister-designate of the new State of Israel, was dispatching cables to other governments asking for recognition. And while the United States, with Harry S. Truman in the White House, was the first to recognize the new nation on May 15, 1948, and the Soviet Union followed three days later, the question on everyone's mind was whether 1 million Jews had any chance fighting against a total Arab population of 40 million.

Estimates vary widely, but it is generally accepted that the combined Arab military strength and resources far outweighed those of the Israelis. British Prime Minister Clement Attlee predicted Israel's doom. His biographer quoted him as saying, "If war broke out between Jews and Arabs, the Foreign Office and the British Chiefs of Staff reported categorically, the Arabs would throw the Jews into the sea."

Even David Ben-Gurion, Israeli prime minister, was gloomy. In proclaiming the State of Israel at a special session of the Jewish National Council of Palestine in Tel Aviv, Ben-Gurion admitted he was not in a celebratory mood. "I feel no gaiety in me," he said, "only deep anxiety, as on the 29th of November, when I was like a mourner at the feast." He referred to the day of the United Nations' resolution that partitioned Palestine into Jewish and Palestinian territories.

David Ben-Gurion (*standing, center*) called for the fulfillment of the Balfour Decla-ration and the 1947 UN Partition Plan, urging the establishment of separate Jewish and Arab states in Palestine. In 1948 he declared the independence of Israel and became the new country's first prime minister.

ARAB CHIEFS OF STAFF
DECLARE WAR AGAINST ISRAEL

Arab chiefs of staff had held a meeting in Damascus in April 1948 to work out a coordinated offensive against Israel. According to the plan, Syrian and Lebanese armies were to invade northern Palestine and occupy Tiberias, Safed, and Nazareth. The main effort would be launched by the Iraqi army and the Arab Legion of Jordan south of Lake Tiberias. They would then move west toward the port of Haifa, which was seen as the main objective of the opening phase of the campaign. The Egyptians, including the Saudi Arabia contingent, were to pin down the Jewish forces south of Tel Aviv.

The plan looked good on paper, but in the field, chaos reigned.

King Abdullah of Jordan was supposed to be the overall commander of the Arab forces, but only his Arab Legion, the most efficient of all the armies, paid any attention to his orders. The Arab Legion was an elite force trained and equipped by the British with a British officer, Sir John Glubb ("Glubb Pasha") in command.

The other Arab armies went their own ways.

Abdullah had no interest in Haifa, which he felt was outside the territory of the Palestinian partition. He had aspired to rule a greater Syria that would have included Palestine and wanted rail access to Haifa, as Transjordan had no Mediterranean port. He had been warned by British Foreign Minister Ernest Bevin, "Don't go and invade the area allotted to the Jews." Abdullah took the warning seriously because he wanted to maintain good relations with the British, who still exerted a major influence on his country even though their mandate had expired.

Abdullah kept his forces in the West Bank territory designated by the United Nations for the Arab State, and surrounded Jerusalem, which had been declared an international city. (Arab Legion forces did occupy East Jerusalem.)

There was no coordinated attack. The Arab offensive was piecemeal, and most Arab regimes committed only some of their armies to Palestine. This greatly diminished the potential for Arab superiority in numbers and armament.

The Syrians attacked in the Jordan Valley in brigade strength, with an armored-car battalion, an artillery regiment, and a company of tanks. The valley was an area of heavy Jewish settlement. The Syrians captured the town of Zemah and, on May 20, attacked the Israeli settlement of Degania.

Degania was defended initially by only 70 men, armed with mortars and machine guns (and no tanks) and using Molotov cocktails against the Syrian tanks. The Syrian force also had some air support, but the bombers were so inaccurate they did not have much effect on the battle.

Israel's military commander, Moshe Dayan, set about bolstering the defensive line facing the Syrians. The Syrians attacked shortly after 4 A.M., but their tanks were knocked out by the Israelis' antitank bazookas and Molotov cocktails. Later, 65-mm guns arrived and began shelling the Syrian positions in Zemah. The supporting Syrian infantry, concealed in a barley field, heard the shriek of Israeli shells over their heads and fled in panic.

The Syrians evacuated Zemah. On an inspection tour the night of the battle, Dayan found that the fleeing Syrians had left behind weapons and vehicles scattered in the streets. "The battle was over," Dayan wrote, "a tough, tragic and depressing battle. Much young blood had been shed, the blood not of trained and experienced veteran warriors but of youngsters meeting death wide-eyed." A truce agreement brokered by the United Nations ended the fighting temporarily in June 1948, but when it expired on July 9 there was renewed fighting between Israel and Egypt in the Negev Desert for ten days.

A final battle took place when the Israelis invaded the Sinai, held by Egypt. Ben-Gurion's reasoning in attacking the Sinai was to push the Egyptians further away from the Israeli capital of Tel Aviv. This brought a strong reaction from Great Britain, which had a treaty with Egypt dating back to 1936.

During the fighting, British Royal Air Force planes flew over Israeli-held territory on reconnaissance, and five of them were shot down by the Israelis. For a time, it almost looked as if Great Britain and Israel would be at war.

The Egyptians turned away Great Britain's help—ironically, the Egyptians wanted to oust British troops from their own country—and negotiated a treaty with Israel. This encouraged the other Arab countries to also seek armistice agreements. Most of them were negotiated without much problem through the UN's special envoy to the region, Ralph Bunche.

When the 1947 UN Partition Plan was created, Tel Aviv was a city of 230,000 people and was slated for inclusion in the Jewish state. With the rejection of the plan and Israel's declaration of independence in 1948, Egypt bombed Tel Aviv but the Egyptians were quickly quashed. Pictured is Tel Aviv after a bombing in June 1948.

Unfortunately, the talks with Syria bogged down because Syria wanted to retain some Israeli territory it still occupied along its border. Negotiations dragged into the summer of 1949. They were held in a stiflingly hot tent pitched on the Tiberias-Damascus highway, near a no-man's land between the two camps.

After long argument, the Syrians agreed to withdraw their forces from Israeli territory on condition that a demilitarized zone be established there. The Israelis agreed, and an armistice was signed in July 1949. Trouble started again when the Israelis insisted on continuing with some water resource development projects they had started, resulting in extensive digging and engineering that spilled over into the demilitarized zone.

Syria objected and complained to the UN that Israel had no right to work in that zone. When the Syrians received no satisfaction from the UN, they began taking potshots across the border at workers in the zone. The UN Security Council passed a resolution calling for work to be suspended pending negotiations, which dragged on without resolution for years.

ARAB NATIONS LOSE THE WAR

Overall, the armistice agreements between Israel and its Arab neighbors were hailed as a triumph for the United Nations, and many observers saw peaceful years ahead. Nevertheless, the sacred city of Jerusalem was left divided and would remain a subject of dispute for the years ahead.

The Arabs in general still resented the Jewish presence in what they considered their state. The peace treaties with Israel were a severe blow to Arab pride. For one thing, most Arab governments controlled the press in their countries, and the general population had been led to believe that the mighty Arab armies would run the Jews out of the region with little difficulty. The Arabs were shocked when they finally learned the truth—that Israel had staved off five powerful Arab countries and remained in solid control of the cherished region.

The year 1948 was called *al-nakba*, Arabic for "catastrophe," in the Arab countries, and those deemed responsible for it were made to suffer. In Egypt, Premier Nokrashy Pasha was assassinated at the end of December. King Farouk was ousted by a military coup three years later, most likely for unrelated reasons.

At the time, King Abdullah of Jordan actually fared better than the other Arab leaders. In 1950, he merged Transjordan and the Arab-held part of Palestine, including the Old City of Jerusalem (now the West Bank), into the Hashemite Kingdom of Jordan. (The Hashemites were a family that traced its lineage back to the Prophet Muhammad.) Syria, and in fact most of the Arab states, never recognized this annexation. On July 20, 1951, Abdullah was assassinated after Friday prayers at the mosque of al-Aqsa in the Old City.

In Syria, the first of many military coups was launched by Colonel Husni Zaim, the head of the Syrian army, who ousted the government of Shukri al-Quwatli. The military blamed Quwatli for losing the war, and he went into exile in Egypt. Thus began more years of turmoil for Syria, which actually had been in ferment almost since the French had pulled out in 1946.

6

The Arabs Unite

Syria had actually been in political turmoil since Evacuation Day in 1946. Before then, the country had been fairly stable with outside enemies to struggle against. In modern times, there had been the Ottoman Empire, then the French, then the Israelis. Faced with a common enemy, the many religious and political factions in the country had managed to unite. Yet, when their primary enterprise became governing themselves, things fell apart. After the French pulled out in 1946, Syria tried a parliamentary democracy. In such a system, a prime minister runs the country and is answerable to a parliament, which makes the laws. It is somewhat similar to the American Congress.

At the time of the French withdrawal, the major political party was the National Bloc, made up of leading members of landowning families and other well-off individuals. They had been educated in French and Turkish universities or at French- and American-operated colleges in Lebanon and Egypt, and they tended to be a bit snobbish. These leaders, mostly large landowners or businessmen, had almost no contact with ordinary citizens and seemed uninterested in their needs.

By mid-1947, two other political parties had risen to prominence—the National Party and the People's Party. The National Party tended to be pro-Egyptian, while the People's Party favored close ties with the Hashemite monarchies in Iraq and Jordan.

FORMATION OF THE BA'ATH PARTY

Yet another party was evolving, one that eventually would dominate the country. The Ba'ath Party was formed in 1940 by

In 1948, Arab authorities called for all feuds between Arabs to come to an end while "the greater feud of Arab against Jew" continued. Here, two Arab families shake hands and celebrate the end of their blood feud.

Michel Aflaq and Salah ad-Din Bitar. *Ba'ath* means "resurrection" in Arabic. The party was made up of students, teachers, professionals, and public employees. They made up Syria's growing middle class. The emergence of a middle class was becoming instrumental in changing Syrian society, as this class became increasingly articulate and influential.

Probably because it was composed of too many idealists and thinkers, the Ba'ath Party didn't have much influence in Syria in its early stages. Its motto was, "Unity, Freedom, and Socialism." "Unity" referred to a united Arab nation, and it was one of the party's guiding principles (and, indeed, a guiding principle of almost all Syrians).

Gradually, the party expanded its membership to include representatives of the lower-middle class. The party saw socialism—government ownership of business—not as an end in itself but as a means of attaining economic and social justice for all.

The Arab superstate envisioned by the Ba'athists was to be based on a secular, rather than a religious, system. This didn't sit well with conservative Sunni religious leaders, although it appealed to minority groups such as Christians and Alawis. The composition of such a superstate was not exactly of pressing interest, since—although the youth thought it would come about in their lifetimes—the possibility of such a creation was highly unlikely.

The Ba'athists liked the Marxist concept of an egalitarian society, but didn't care for communism. Members felt that the communists were too closely allied with the Soviet Union, and the Ba'athists opposed alignment with any of the superpowers.

The fight against Israel in 1948 united the country once again as it dealt with a common enemy. After the war, the military, angered at what it saw as civilian corruption that had been instrumental in losing the war, ousted the civilian government of Shukri al-Quwatli.

It was a bloodless coup d'état staged by Colonel Husni Zaim, a Kurd whom some observers think was brought to power by the American CIA. The takeover was applauded by the press and most members of the public because it seemed to mean a permanent transfer of power from the traditional landowning elite to a new coalition of young intellectuals, army officers, and the growing middle class.

On August 14, 1949, Zaim was ousted by a military coup engineered by Colonel Sami Hinnawi. He ordered Zaim and his prime minister, Muhsinal-Barazi, to be arrested, and both were executed. Hinnawi initiated closer ties with the Hashemites in Jordan and Iraq. He was suspected of planning a union between Syria and Iraq, which disturbed certain forces in the army, and he was arrested by another Kurd, Colonel Adib Shishakli, who then proceeded to impose his own military dictatorship on the country.

SYRIA BECOMES A REPUBLIC

Shishakli formed his own party, the Arab Liberation Movement. In July 1953, Syrians approved a new constitution making Syria a presidential republic rather than a parliamentary one. Shishakli was named president. He seemed to favor the West, but also clamped down on nearly all of Syria's political parties. When the Druzes staged a rebellion, Shishakli declared martial law and bombed the Druzes in their homeland in southern Syria. The patience of his opponents ran out, and Shishakli was ousted in Syria's fourth coup on February 25, 1954.

Shishakli fled to Brazil, where he was assassinated in 1964 by a Druze in retaliation for the earlier bombing.

Meanwhile, the National Party and the People's Party were gradually losing influence—a reflection of the changing power balance among the classes of Syrian society. To add to the confusion of political parties vying for power, two more left-wing parties came along—the Syrian Social Nationalist Party (SSNP) and the Arab Socialist Party (ASP). Furthermore, the Syrian Communist Party (SCP) was making itself heard. This was perhaps a reflection of a growing Soviet influence in Syria.

The Ba'ath Party was strengthened in 1953 when it merged with the Arab Socialist Party. The members of these parties did not merely engage in polite discussions, as the American political parties do. They tended to get violent. For instance, in April 1955, Colonel Adnan Malik, deputy chief of staff and a leading Ba'athist, was assassinated by a sergeant in the SSNP. This brought about the end of the SSNP in Syria, however, as its members were accused of trying to overthrow the government. They either were arrested or fled the country.

In 1957, the Ba'athists entered into a partnership with the Communist Party in an effort to crush conservative opposition, but it backfired. The communists, while small in number, were well-disciplined and determined. They came to dominate the new partnership and the Ba'ath Party started to lose influence.

UNITED ARAB REPUBLIC

In order to rid itself of the communists, the Ba'ath Party drafted a bill in 1957 calling for union with Egypt. No one dared oppose the bill because Arab unity was an almost sacred idea. The Ba'athists knew that Egyptian President Gamal Abdel Nasser opposed the concept of political parties and was in the process of persecuting the communists in his own country. So Syria and Egypt created the United Arab Republic (UAR) in 1958. It is widely believed, in Egypt especially, that the Syrians pressured Nasser to create this organic union, widely hailed at the time as a first step toward complete Arab unification. That effort also backfired.

Akram al-Hawrani, founder of the Arab Socialist Party, and now head of the Ba'ath Party, was appointed vice president of the new republic. Nasser, of course, was president. The Ba'athists saw the ascension of Hawrani to a position of power as a sign that they would have a major influence on the new nation. They were wrong.

Syria soon realized it had virtually become a colony of Egypt, and many people wanted out of the UAR. On September 28, 1961, a military coup did just that, and Syria went back to independence. The country formed a short-lived new government with a constituent assembly composed mostly of members of the conservative People's Party and National Party. People's Party leader Nazim al-Qudsi was elected president.

Syria was plunged into a state of near anarchy in 1961, during the 18 months following the breakup of the UAR. There were coups and countercoups; street fighting between Nasserites, who wanted to return to union with Egypt, and communists and Ba'athists; as well as battles between rival army factions. The country was in chaos.

This ended in 1963 when a group of senior army officers staged another coup. These army officers, who had used the Ba'ath Party to gain power, soon abandoned its democratic principles and established a military dictatorship. They had organized a secret military committee during the merger with Egypt with the aim of seizing power in the UAR. After the country pulled out of the alliance, the officers turned their attention to taking control in Syria.

Although there were efforts made at unity talks with Egypt and Iraq in the spring of 1963, these officers had little time

Major-General Abel Karem Zahreddin, commander of the Syrian army, announces the formation of People's Courts to try former members of the Syrian government. The army staged a coup two days before on March 28, 1963.

for Arab unity. They favored Syrian nationalism. Most of the committee members belonged to minority religious groups. The original core of conspirators consisted of three Alawis and two Ismailis (who were, like the Alawis, a Shiite sect). Later, the group was enlarged to 15 members. It then included six Sunni Muslims (the majority sect in Syria), five Alawis, two Druzes, and two Ismailis.

The 1963 coup was seen as a crucial turning point in Syria's history since its independence from France. The focus of Syrian politics shifted to the left, where it remained. Aflaq and Bitar, the Ba'ath Party founders, were expelled from the party. (Aflaq was assassinated in Paris in 1980, presumably by Syrian intelligence agents.) In 1966, the rise of so-called neo-Ba'athists to power presaged the growing struggle with Israel, which would lead to outright war in June 1967.

7

The Six-Day War

During his tenure, Egyptian leader Gamal Abdel Nasser frequently rattled his country's sabers, aided by a well-developed but not always informative press and radio station. He was openly hostile to Israel and pushed hard for Arab unity. However, Nasser was not able to sustain his threats and claims. For example, when he was angered because the United States withdrew its offer to finance the Aswan Dam, a project crucial to Egypt's economic development, Nasser nationalized the Suez Canal Company on July 26, 1956.

Great Britain was furious. It relied on the canal for transportation of its oil imports and other crucial goods. In an effort to destabilize Nasser, it helped create a plan in which Israel would attack Egypt in the Sinai, followed by Great Britain and France attacking Egypt directly.

On October 29, Israel launched its attack with a paratroop drop deep inside the Sinai. Moshe Dayan—a renowned Israeli military leader, instantly recognizable by his eye patch—led the Israeli forces. Within eight days, the Israelis drove the Egyptian army out of the desert. Israel claimed it entered Egypt to attack bases used by the fedayeen terrorists. (*Fedayeen* means "people who sacrifice themselves for a cause.")

U.S. President Dwight Eisenhower urged Israel to pull out of the Sinai after it took care of the fedayeen bases. The Israeli prime minister, David Ben-Gurion, ignored him. Great Britain and France then called on Egypt and Israel to pull back from the Suez Canal.

General Moshe Dayan *(standing)*, Israeli soldier and minister of defense, holds a press conference during the Six-Day War in 1967. During the years following the war, Dayan enjoyed enormous popularity and was considered a potential candidate for prime minister. For 25 years he was a prominent figure in Israel's wars and, more than anyone, exemplified Israel's determination to survive.

EGYPT ATTACKED

When Egypt refused, as the allies expected it to, Great Britain and France attacked Egypt on November 6. The attack angered the United States, and it also angered the Soviet Union, which was backing Egypt in the fight (and which had sold Egypt and Syria millions of dollars' worth of weaponry). In fact, the Soviets threatened to annihilate Israel if it failed to withdraw its forces from the Sinai.

The Soviet leadership was mostly just making threats, but President Eisenhower was furious. This was mainly because the United States had not been informed in advance of the attack on Egypt. He led the pack in the United Nations that demanded Great Britain and France end their attack. The American president also threatened economic sanctions against Great Britain if it did not withdraw from Egypt. President Eisenhower came to realize that he had been duped by his longtime allies.

The war ended quickly, but for a time the world had been on the edge of its seat.

Nasser's prestige continued to grow after King Faisal was overthrown in Iraq by Brigadier Karim Qassem on July 14, 1958. Faisal was murdered, along with members of his family and a number of government officials. The revolution resulted from a rising tide of pro-Nasser feeling in the Arab world. Shortly before the Iraqi revolution, Syria had joined Egypt in the United Arab Republic (UAR), and Nasser was again riding high.

In a short time, however, things started to go very wrong. First, Qassem decided he did not need Nasser; Iraq would go its own way. Qassem did not want to share Iraq's oil revenues with the UAR. In fact, Baghdad radio began insulting the Egyptian president. Then Syria pulled out of the United Arab Republic in September 1961, and Damascus radio started criticizing Nasser as well.

Another debacle occurred in September 1962, when Nasser sent a large body of troops into Yemen. Some Yemeni army officers had overthrown the imam (Muslim religious leader) there, and Egypt's troops were sent to help the officers. Meanwhile, the Saudis sent aid to the deposed imam, who resisted the Egyptian and Yemeni "republicans." That ended in a humiliating disaster when the troops got bogged down and had to return home five years later, shortly after Egypt's defeat in the 1967 conflict.

Nasser was also the target of increasing criticism from Arab countries, including Syria, for not taking a hard enough line on Israel. The Syrians were openly hostile to Israel, and the Soviet Union backed them. Thus emerged one of the early confrontations in the Cold War—between the Soviets, backing Syria, and the United States, backing Israel. Something had to give. Nasser found himself deluged with abuse and mockery, to such an extent that his own people were beginning to look at him askance. This was especially true in the spring of 1967, after the neo-Ba'athists had taken power in Syria. Even Jordan was mocking Nasser.

A THREAT TO SYRIA

The Soviet ambassador to Egypt told Nasser that the Israelis planned to attack Syria on May 13, 1967. That was not true, but it obliged Nasser to make a decision. If the Israelis crushed Syria and Nasser did nothing, he would be seen as a traitor to the Arab cause. Nasser very publicly mobilized his armed forces and sent them through the Sinai toward Israel's border.

Nasser then announced that he was closing the Straits of Tiran and the Gulf of Aqaba to Israeli shipping, as well as to all ships carrying goods to Israel. Nasser also continued to make bellicose statements. At one point he said, "They, the Jews, threaten war; we tell them: Welcome. We are ready for war."

Israeli Prime Minister Levi Eshkol and his foreign minister, Abba Eban, tried to enlist help from the United States and other powers. He was rebuffed by French President Charles de Gaulle. The British were sympathetic, but made no firm offers of help.

American President Lyndon Johnson spoke of a possible "international naval force" to open the blockades, but it never happened. The United States did send some ships through the canal, but its real problem was having a half million men tied down at the time in Vietnam.

The lengthy delay in responding to the Arab threat was met with anger by the Israeli military, and joy by Israel's Arab enemies. It seemed that Nasser had won a political victory and that the Israelis were afraid to fight.

Jordan's King Hussein went to Cairo and placed his armed forces under Egyptian command. The radio stations of the Arab world stopped attacking one another and concentrated their venom on Israel.

With the appointment of the military leader Moshe Dayan as their minister for defense, the Israelis were clearly ready for war. Nasser actually was reluctant to go to war with Israel, chiefly because his best troops were tied down in Yemen at the time. He knew the Israelis were tough. To stop hostilities, he would have to open the Straits of Tiran for Israeli shipping, and that he could not do. He was trapped by his own rhetoric.

The rest of the Arab world, including Syria, was more than ready to go to war. Its armies, along with those of Jordan and Iraq, had been massing troops along the Israeli border for some months. Total Arab strength, at least on paper, vastly outnumbered that of Israel. The Arabs had twice as many troops, more than three times as many tanks, and more than three times as many combat aircraft.

ARAB COUNTRIES TAUNT ISRAEL

Taunts and threats from the Arab countries were getting strident. One rabble-rouser, Ahmad Al-Shukairy, then head of the Palestine Liberation Organization (PLO), declared, "Those native-born Israelis who will survive the war will be permitted to remain in the country. But I don't think many will survive."

Nasser matched Shukairy's aggressive rhetoric, proclaiming that the very existence of Israel "was in itself an act of aggression."

Syrian defense minister Hafez al-Assad, future president of Syria, declared, "The army, which has long been preparing itself for the battle and has a finger on the trigger, demands in a single voice that the battle be expedited. . . . The time [has] come to wage the liberation battle."

The Arabs were soon to get all the war they wanted.

THE SIX-DAY WAR BEGINS

It was fitting that the coded order for Israel's attack on Egypt was "Nashonim, action!" Nashon was the leader of the tribe of Judah in the Biblical story of Exodus when the Jews were led out of slavery in Egypt by Moses. Nashon was traditionally believed to have been the first to enter the waters of the Red Sea after God parted them.

It was June 5, 1967, 7:45 A.M.

Moshe Dayan was in the Israeli Air Force command center, watching the war table before him. When word came that Israeli war planes had made it undetected to Egyptian airfields, the order went out to the armored divisions elsewhere on the nation's threatened borders to start moving.

The Six-Day War, in which Israeli forces defeated the armies of Egypt, Jordan, and Syria in less than a week, had begun.

Israeli planes pounced on Egyptian airfields, catching most of the planes still on the ground. Between 7:14 A.M. and 8:55 A.M., 11 Egyptian airfields were attacked and 197 Egyptian aircraft were destroyed—189 on the ground and eight in dogfights in the air. Six airfields were completely knocked out—four in Sinai and two west of the Suez Canal—and 16 radar stations were put out of action.

That was only the first wave. In the second wave, 164 planes attacked 14 air bases and destroyed 107 more Egyptian aircraft. The Israelis lost 11 pilots; six were killed, two taken prisoner, and three wounded. Nine planes were lost.

The Syrian, Jordanian, and Iraqi air forces launched their attacks on Israel unaware of the destruction of the Egyptian aircraft. Twelve Russian-made MiG-17s took off from Damascus at 11:50 A.M. Two of them attacked Kibbutz Degania, where Dayan had grown up, setting fire to a silo and a poultry run. The Syrian

Pictured are Egyptian aircraft destroyed on the ground in an Israeli pre-emptive strike during the Six-Day War in 1967.

planes then went on to attack—and miss—an Israeli stronghold at Bet Yerach, on the Sea of Galilee, and a dam on the Jordan River.

Syria continued to attack, but inflicted minimal damage on Israel. Meanwhile, Syria lost almost 50 percent of its air force—53 planes destroyed out of a total of 112—thanks to Israeli attacks on the Syrian air bases of Damir, Damascus, Seikal, Marjarial, and T-4.

Other Arab countries did equally poorly in the air. Jordanian planes took off at noon and attacked the coastal resort of Netanya and the Kfar Syrkin airfield near Petach Tikvah. They destroyed only a Nord transport plane on the ground at Kfar Syrkin.

Two hours later, three Iraqi planes fired rockets in the direction of the settlement at Nahalal, no doubt believing it was the Ramat David airfield. They caused no damage and returned to Iraq.

Jordan and Iraq paid dearly for these attacks. Israeli planes destroyed the entire Jordanian air force of 28 planes in attacks on the two Jordanian air bases of Mafrak and Amman. Iraq lost 10 planes in a three-sortie attack on one field, called 3-H.

In Egypt, Cairo Radio was bragging that the Egyptian Air Force had shot down 40 Israeli planes. There was no truth to that, of course, but it was typical of the way the Egyptians were deluding themselves that they were having an easy time with the Israeli forces. In reality, they were being crushed.

Sinai was cleared of Egyptian forces in fierce fighting. Israeli troops smashed their way to the Suez Canal. After four days of battle, Nasser accepted a cease-fire.

Meanwhile, Israeli forces were dealing with King Hussein's Jordanian army at the divided city of Jerusalem. The Jordanians were soon subdued, and Israel had control of Jerusalem for the first time since it was divided after the 1948 war. The Israelis were now able to turn their full attention to their last remaining enemy—Syria.

Syria had resisted Egypt's plea that it launch an all-out attack on Israel. Except for a few bombing sorties that didn't really hit anything, the Syrians set up a defensive strategy with occasional forays into Israeli territory. Syria cancelled what had been called "Operation Nasser" in favor of "Operation Jihad (Holy War)," implying a period of Muslim, as opposed to secular, influence. Along with its brief and generally unsuccessful attacks across the border, Syria now concentrated on shelling a northern kibbutz and army camps.

SYRIA LOSES THE GOLAN HEIGHTS

On June 9, Israeli troops and armor attacked the Syrian positions on the border and captured the Golan Heights. The Syrians commanded the high ground there and were able to fire down on the advancing Israelis, but Israeli troops were able to gain command of the Syrian positions by nightfall. The loss of the strategic and symbolic Golan Heights was a bitter disappointment for the Syrians.

Israeli air support also helped to turn the tide of battle. In the northern part of Golan, Syrians held out heroically against the enemy. Dayan wrote, "The Syrian force at Zaoura put up a stubborn defense and fought well. But it was soon overcome."

Another difficult battle took place at Tel Faher, and again Syrian troops fought fiercely. Yet, on Saturday, June 10, advancing Israelis found the Syrian positions empty. The Syrians had abandoned them during the night, leaving antitank guns and heavy and light machine guns behind.

The Syrians retreated toward Damascus, 40 miles away. Fearing that the Israelis would march on the capital, the government instructed its United Nations delegates to urge the Security Council to adopt a cease-fire resolution.

The Israelis set up a frontier between them and the Syrians that included a large piece of Syrian territory. The Israelis now commanded the high ground, with a clear view of the plain stretching toward Damascus.

"In their mind's eye," Dayan wrote of the Syrians, "they would see us getting into our tanks and galloping on to Damascus whenever the fancy should take us. This may have been thought a flight of Oriental fantasy, but anyone going up to the Golan Heights and seeing the vast plain stretching away toward Damascus could hardly rule out such a possibility."

Among those made nervous by that possibility were the Soviets. In fact, the Soviets warned the United States that if the United States did not stop the Israeli advance, the Soviets would intervene on behalf of the Syrians. After all, the Soviets had invested a lot, militarily and politically, in Syria.

Diplomatic cables flashed around the world. The Israelis told the United States that they had no intention of advancing any farther. Their only intention, they said, was to put their settlements out of artillery range.

ISRAEL CAPTURES MORE ARAB TERRITORY

In the swift war, the Israelis captured the Sinai Peninsula from Egypt; occupied the east bank of the Suez Canal, shutting it down; and took the West Bank and Jerusalem from Jordan and the Golan Heights from Syria.

Emotionally, the capture of the Old City of Jerusalem was the high point of the war for Israel. Jews were now able to visit and pray at the Western Wall of Herod's Temple. This had been impossible while it was held by the Jordanians.

The occupation by Israel of Egyptian and Syrian territories sowed the seeds for future violence among those countries. For the Syrians, the loss of Golan was to become a sore point for decades to come. The question of its return to Syria would influence all of the country's decisions about relations with Israel and cause upheaval within Syria itself.

8

A Region Divided

The Syrian government in the 1960s was a bewildering and fast-changing array of faces. Just as one man or faction attained power, another man or faction soon seized power. Nevertheless, the changes of government, however abrupt, were usually accomplished without the shedding of blood.

Just before the Six-Day War, there had been frequent changes of government because of a struggle that began in 1964 between the centrist and leftist wings of the dominant Ba'ath Party. (Left-wingers tended to be more radically socialist and the right-wingers more conservative. The centrists were, of course, in the middle.)

On July 17 and 18, 1963, some 2,000 Syrian Nasserites—supporters of the president of Egypt—had attempted a coup. It was crushed by the military after heavy fighting in Damascus. Major General Amin al-Hafiz, commander in chief of the armed forces, emerged as the country's newest strongman.

This was the first time that a coup or coup attempt in Syria had led to violence and loss of life. Justice for the rebels was swift. Eight army officers and twelve civilians involved in the uprising were convicted in summary trials before revolutionary security courts and executed by firing squads the same day.

Hafiz later became prime minister and held a number of other government posts before he was ousted in another bloody coup on February 23, 1966. That coup was engineered by two Ba'athist generals, Salah al-Jadid and Hafez al-Assad, both members of the Muslim Alawi sect. Hafiz, wounded in the fighting, was arrested and jailed. Assad, the future president of Syria, was named minister of defense. (He would be still holding the post when the Six-Day War broke out.)

In the fall of 1966 a military countercoup led by a Druze, Salim Hatum, failed when Assad threatened to send the air force after Hatum's forces. Hatum and his associates fled to Jordan, but he came back in June 1967, saying he wanted to fight against Israel. He was shot.

Then came the Arab world's traumatic defeat in the Six-Day War. It discredited the radical socialist regimes of both Nasser's Egypt and Ba'athist Syria. As a result, the defeat had the effect of strengthening the hands of the moderates and rightists in the Ba'ath Party and became the catalyst for Assad's rise to power.

Meanwhile, the great powers continued to view activities in the Middle East through the prism of the Cold War. Both the United States and the Soviet Union tended to see every major crisis there as the result of a sinister plot by the other side to gain power and influence in the region.

GLOBALISTS VS. REGIONALISTS

In the United States, there was a continuing debate between the "globalists" and the "regionalists" in dealing with the Middle East. The globalists regarded the conflicts as a struggle for supremacy between the United States and the Soviet Union. The regionalists saw the problems as more local and tried to figure out how the United States could help solve them.

The State of Israel was at the core of the debate. The globalists viewed Israel as an asset because it countered Soviet influence on the Arab countries. The regionalists tended to see Israel as a liability, contending that supporting Israel opened the door to Soviet intervention on the side of the Arabs and prevented America from having constructive dealings with the Arabs.

The Israel-first school of thought dominated American policy after the 1967 war. For one thing, Americans, both Jews and non-Jews, admired the Israelis. They liked their pioneering spirit, because they thought it was that same spirit that built

America. They also admired Israeli courage, their fighting abilities, and their democratic ways in a region that did not see much democracy. In addition, American politicians had to deal with a powerful pro-Israeli lobby on its own soil and the equally potent and usually unified Jewish vote.

The first meeting of the Arab states after the Six-Day War occurred from August 19 to September 1, 1967, at Khartoum. The meeting produced the famous "three no's"—no peace with Israel, no recognition of Israel, and no negotiations with Israel concerning any Palestinian territory. It was a victory for those who subscribed to the regionalist theory.

RESOLUTION 242

On November 22, 1967, the United Nations asserted itself in the Middle East with Security Council Resolution 242, which called for Israel to withdraw its armed forces "from territories occupied in the recent conflict." It called on the Arabs to end their belligerence and recognize Israel's right to live peacefully within secure and recognized boundaries.

The resolution was subject to different interpretations. The Arabs thought it meant that the Israelis should immediately pull out of the territories it had taken in the Six-Day War. To the Israelis, the resolution meant negotiations should begin, leading to formal peace treaties that included establishing those "secure and recognized boundaries." The American government interpreted it to mean there should be minor adjustments in the western frontier of the West Bank, demilitarization measures in the Sinai and the Golan Heights, and a fresh look at the status of Jerusalem as part of the peace settlement that the United States had wanted, at least under Lyndon Johnson.

United States President Richard M. Nixon and his national security adviser, Henry Kissinger, were globalists. Their policy was simply to explore ways to expel the Soviet Union from the Middle East. This would not involve committing troops, as in the conflict in Vietnam, but supporting local U.S. allies. These

In 1967, the United Nations Security Council *(above)*, released Security Council Resolution 242, a statement establishing the necessary steps toward peace in the Middle East. The resolution, however, was vaguely worded and interpreted in various ways by several countries.

included, besides Israel, Turkey, Iran, and Saudi Arabia. There-fore, America offered Israel diplomatic support, economic assis-tance, and arms on an ever-growing scale.

In 1969, another crisis occurred that would test the patience of both globalists and regionalists. Nasser, frustrated by the standstill on dealing with the problem of Israel, launched what became known as the War of Attrition.

THE WAR OF ATTRITION

This so-called war was at first a duel of artillery fire across the Suez Canal. Egypt hoped to dislodge the Israelis from the Sinai. The Israelis responded by bombing Egypt. They believed they would have American support because the War of Attrition would gradually bleed Israel to death. Syria was not directly involved, although Damascus did, of course, aid the cause of the Palestinian fedayeen.

Nasser dashed off to Moscow to get Soviet help. He demanded surface-to-air missiles and Russian crews to operate them. To Soviet Premier Leonid Brezhnev, he said, "I am a leader who is bombed every day in his own country, whose army is exposed and whose people are naked. I have the courage to tell our peo-ple the unfortunate truth—that, whether they like it or not, the Americans are masters of the world."

Hearing this, the Soviets agreed to give Nasser everything he asked for, and more.

On July 30, Israeli fighters shot down four Soviet planes near the Suez Canal. The next day, the government of Israel agreed to accept a cease-fire and the application of the United Nations' Resolution 242. Golda Meir, then prime minister of Israel, "had at last jammed on the brakes, very near to the edge of the cliff," writes Conor Cruise O'Brien in his book, *The Siege*.

The Meir government dragged its feet in negotiating a peace with Egypt. Nasser died and Anwar Sadat took over. Sadat was more amenable to negotiations than his hot-headed predecessor.

Still, no progress was made, and it became increasingly clear that more bloodshed was in store for the region.

Meanwhile, Syria was highly critical of Jordan and Lebanon for their efforts to control Palestinian guerrillas in their territories. Indeed, Syria tried to make the Lebanese and Jordanian governments allow the fedayeen to operate against Israel from their territories. At the same time, the Syrians kept a tight lid on terrorist activities in their own country. They were especially watchful of the radical As Saiqa ("Thunderbolt"). As Saiqa was not allowed to use Syria as a base for attacks on Israel for fear of Israeli reprisals.

BLACK SEPTEMBER

In September 1970, the Jordanian army launched attacks on camps on Jordanian soil belonging to the radical Palestine Liberation Organization (PLO) and on Palestinian refugee camps that were under the control of PLO units near Amman. This offensive became known to the PLO as "Black September." Syria sent about 200 tanks to aid the PLO forces. Meanwhile, Iraqi troops gathered on the Jordanian border but did not enter the country.

The world was so alarmed by these activities that the United States sent its 6th Fleet to the eastern Mediterranean. As part of the Cold War mentality of the day, the United States was convinced that the Soviet Union was behind the crisis. The Syrian tanks came under heavy fire by Jordanian troops and warplanes, and were forced to withdraw.

This failure of the Syrian intervention could be traced back to the same domestic political disagreements within the Ba'ath leadership that were disrupting the country internally. The Jadid faction of the party wanted full support of the PLO in Jordan and participation in its activities. Assad and his associates opposed such action. Assad had refused to send his air force to support the tanks in Jordan, primarily because he feared a devastating attack from Israel.

SYRIA IS UNSETTLED

On November 13, 1970, Jadid was out. Army units arrested him and his associates. Three days later, the regional command of the Ba'ath Party issued a statement saying the change that had occurred was merely a transfer of power within the party. A new party congress was to be convened to reorganize the party; a national front government was to be organized under the new Ba'athist leadership, and a people's council, or legislature, was to be formed. The statement also affirmed continued support for the Palestinian cause.

Three days after that, Ahmad al-Khatib was named acting chief of staff and Assad prime minister and minister of defense. (Khatib was a figurehead who served only four months; his role was then filled by Assad.) Assad claimed the change in government was not a coup. He called it a "correction movement."

By the end of the 1960s, Syria was at odds with its Arab neighbors. The Ba'athist Party in Syria was fighting with the Ba'athist Party in Iraq. The Syrians felt the Iraqi Ba'athists were trying to interfere with the party in Syria.

Syria and Jordan were smarting over their disputes dealing with the Palestinian Liberation Organization. Within Syria, there was still anger at the Egyptians for the continuing efforts of the Nasserites to influence Syrian policy. Nasser's dream had always been of a pan-Arab nation dominated by Egypt. The Syrians did not like that idea at all.

Syria was angry at the Western powers, especially the United States, for their continued support of Israel, Syria's sworn enemy. And even the Soviets, who had supplied Syria with arms and other goods, were looked on with suspicion. Like many nations, Syria did not like to become too cozy with powerful nations, out of fear that they could be dominated.

Of course, the Syrians were still furious at the Israelis for their occupation of the Golan Heights. This continuing antipathy toward the Israelis led the Syrians to the ill-fated decision to join Egypt in another attack on Israel.

9

The Yom Kippur War and Lebanon Conflicts

Yom Kippur is the holiest day in the Jewish calendar. It is a day of fasting and prayer for forgiveness of sins committed during the year. Jews gather in synagogues on the eve of Yom Kippur when the fast begins, and return the following morning to continue confessing, doing penance, and praying for forgiveness.

The Arab nations chose October 6, the day of Yom Kippur in 1973, to attack Israel. At 2 P.M., Egyptian and Syrian forces attacked at the same time, catching the Israelis by surprise for another war.

The Israelis were not totally unprepared, however. On the Syrian front they had a fighting force of some 180 tanks, 11 artillery batteries, and 5,000 men. On the Egyptian front they had about 275 tanks, 12 artillery batteries, and 8,500 men.

The Israelis were informed that the United States had sent a message to Egypt demanding to know what its intentions were. The United States contacted Syria indirectly, through the Soviet Union. No response came from either country. Both Egypt and Syria had informed the Soviets of their intentions and the Soviets made no effort to change their minds. The Soviets apparently knew ahead of time of the attack, because they pulled their dependents out of Cairo and Damascus two days before.

SYRIA AND EGYPT ATTACK ISRAEL

Syrian aircraft had crossed Israeli air space and Egyptian troops were crossing the Suez Canal on rafts. The Soviets had been

A young Syrian boy plays near military equipment on display at an exhibition at the 6 October Museum in Damascus. The display demonstrates missiles and tanks similar to the ones used in the Yom Kippur War.

equipping and training the armies of both Egypt and Syria for some time. A new shipment of 15 batteries of Russian-made SA-6 (surface-to-air) missiles had been dispatched to Syria and 10 to Egypt. Syria also received Frog-7 surface-to-surface missiles with a range of 40 miles.

In addition, the Soviets had provided both countries with about 500 T-62 tanks, as well as such antitank weapons as Sagger missiles, RPGs (rocket-propelled grenades), and other arms.

The Egyptian offensive opened with an air attack accompanied by an artillery barrage against Israeli forces on the east bank of the Suez Canal. Some 2,000 Egyptian guns opened up along the entire front. In the first minute of the attack, 10,500 shells from medium and heavy artillery and medium and heavy mortars fell on Israeli positions. That amounted to 175 shells per second.

The Frogs—the surface-to-surface missiles—opened up. Tanks rolled up to ramps prepared on the sand ramparts of the canal and began firing. "Over 3,000 tons of concentrated destruction were launched against a handful of Israeli fortifications in a barrage that turned the east bank of the Suez Canal into an inferno in 53 minutes," one observer wrote.

On the northern front, the Syrians launched a similarly devastating attack. Two Israeli brigades came under attack from three Syrian divisions—1,100 tanks against 157 tanks. After 22 hours of fighting, 90 percent of the officers of the Israeli brigades and most of the men were either killed or wounded.

On October 7, the Egyptian 7th Division crossed the Suez Canal with all its forces. A counterattack by the Israelis the next day failed. In three days, Israel lost 50 aircraft and hundreds of tanks. The Israelis called up their reserves and rallied their armies from the Yom Kippur break and were ready to fight back. The Israelis concentrated their attack on the Syrians on the northern front. By October 10, despite initial Israeli setbacks, the Syrians were on the defensive, driven out of the territory they had taken in the opening days of the war.

The next day, Israeli forces invaded Syria. They seemed to be heading for Damascus. This alarmed the Soviets and they began a massive airlift of armaments to Cairo and Damascus. The United States responded with an equally massive airlift of armaments to Israel. Another East–West confrontation was on.

Negotiations had gotten underway between the Americans and the Soviets for a cease-fire that would be ordered by the United Nations. The fighting started up again when Israeli forces surrounded the Egyptian 3rd Army while Syria and Israel were, in the meantime, fighting over Mount Hermon. The Israelis threatened to annihilate the Egyptian Army or starve it out. The result was the most serious confrontation between the United States and the Soviet Union since the Cuban Missile Crisis of 1962. The Soviets made it clear they would not put up with the destruction of Egypt's 3rd Army, and that they would take action to prevent it. The United States put its own military on nuclear red alert.

CEASE-FIRE DECLARED

The matter defused before it came to nuclear war. The confrontation ended when Israel agreed to a cease-fire on October 25, 1973. Thus, the Yom Kippur War (also called the Ramadan War or October War by Arabs) ended in a stalemate, leaving no one satisfied and laying the groundwork for future conflict between Israel and its Arab neighbors.

CIVIL WAR IN LEBANON

One of the more significant of these conflicts took place in Lebanon. In 1975, civil war broke out in Lebanon between Christians and Muslims, with participation by the Palestine Liberation Organization. Each side blamed the other, and Syria most likely was involved from the start. Both Israel and Syria considered intervening. Syrian President Hafez al-Assad, who had assumed power in 1970, knew that a takeover of Lebanon by Muslim forces and the PLO would invite an Israeli attempt to occupy the country.

Syria and Lebanon had a special relationship going back centuries. Syria considered Lebanon part of "Greater Syria" and had considerable influence in the country. Syrians believed that the French had deliberately cut off Lebanon from Syria. Neither the United States nor Israel had any objections to Syrian intervention in Lebanon. The United States would have objected, as the Israelis would have, if Syria had helped the Palestinian or Lebanese Muslims (as they would later).

So, in January 1976, a detachment of 50 Syrian officers was sent to Beirut to help enforce one of a series of cease-fires among the combatants. On March 16, Syria ordered Syrian-backed units of the Palestine Liberation Army (the standing army of the PLO) to stop leftist Muslim forces from attacking the palace of the country's Christian president, Sulayman Franjiyah.

The Syrian presence in Lebanon grew rapidly. On April 9, about 3,000 Syrian regular troops entered the country. In May, the Lebanese parliament elected a new, Syrian-backed Christian president, Elias Sarkis. By the fall, more than 22,000 Syrian troops were in Lebanon.

In June 1978, Christian militiamen assassinated Christian leader Tony Franjiyah, a son of the former president and Syria's staunchest ally in Lebanon. That deed provoked the Syrians into essentially switching sides to favor the Muslims. They began massive artillery barrages on Christian territory in East Beirut.

The Syrians were roundly criticized internationally for attacks that were causing the deaths of innocent civilians. Nevertheless, Syrian troops remained in Lebanon.

ISRAEL ATTACKS LEBANON

In June 1982, Israel and Syria clashed when the Israelis invaded Lebanon to knock out PLO bases that had been used to launch terrorist attacks on Israel. The Israelis at the same time fired on the missile bases Syria had set up in Lebanon's Bekka Valley. On June 9, the Israeli air force attacked the Syrian air-defense system, knocking out 17 SAM-6, SAM-3, and SAM-2 batteries. In a fierce air battle, Israeli planes shot down 25 Syrian planes, without a loss to Israel. Israeli troops besieged Beirut and then marched into the city.

The Syrian and PLO forces were trapped in West Beirut, and the Israelis began shelling them. By August 1982, the Palestinians and Syrians were ready to give up. More than 10,000 men belonging to various PLO units and 4,000 Syrian troops were allowed to pull out of Beirut (though not completely from Lebanon).

ISRAEL AND EGYPT SIGN PEACE TREATY

By this time, Israel and Egypt had signed a peace treaty—on March 27, 1979, in Washington, D.C.—ending 31 years of war. The treaty resulted from the famous Camp David negotiations organized by U.S. President Jimmy Carter. Carter had brought Egyptian President Anwar Sadat and Israeli Prime Minister Menachem Begin together at the presidential retreat in Maryland. After 13 days of tough negotiations, the two sides agreed to certain conditions: Israel would withdraw from the Sinai, and relations between the two countries would be normalized. In addition, the United States agreed to continue its support and to provide economic help as needed.

Syria blamed the Israeli occupation of Lebanon on what it saw as Egypt's defection from the Arab cause by signing a treaty with Israel. The fact was that once Egypt had withdrawn from the Arab coalition, no combination of the other Arab states was strong enough to fight Israel. This explains why Israel could invade Lebanon and push back the Syrians, who got no help from Egypt or any other country.

On August 23, 1982, while the PLO and Syrians were evacuating West Beirut, Bashir Gemayel, a Maronite Christian and leader of the Lebanese Christian Phalangists Party, was elected president of Lebanon. (The Phalangist Party, although officially secular, is supported by Maronites. Its name derives from the same root as the word *phalanx*, meaning "battalion.")

The Syrians were angered. The Damascus newspaper *al-Ba'ath* accused Gemayel of treason against Syria, and declared that the "day of judgment [was] near." It was right. On September 14, 1982, Gemayel was killed by a bomb at a party headquarters building in West Beirut. In Damascus, *al-Ba'ath* praised the killing. The suspect arrested in the bombing, Habib Shartouni, was a member of the Syrian Social Nationalist Party.

The Israeli reaction was to occupy West Beirut "to prevent any possible incident and to secure quiet." The Israelis then made the disastrous decision to let the Christian Phalangists into

Palestinian refugee camps at Sabra and Chatila to clear out any terrorists. The Phalangists proceeded to slaughter men, women, and children in revenge for Bashir's murder. It took them two days to massacre several hundred people.

Bashir Gemayel's brother, Amin, was elected president of Lebanon in 1982. The American president at the time, the newly elected Ronald Reagan, had an ambitious plan for Lebanon. He wanted both Israel and Syria out of the country. Reagan gave a speech in September 1982 proposing a peace plan, but Israel rejected it. It is likely that Syria would have also rejected it.

Israel pulled out of its positions in the Druze area of the Shouf Mountains, but as soon as it left, the Druzes attacked the Christians there and massacred an estimated 17,000 people in Christian villages. Alarmed by the violence, Reagan sent U.S. Marines into Lebanon to help keep order. His position on the Syrians, whose troops remained in Lebanon, was, as he put it, to keep them "on the outside looking in."

U.S. MARINES PULL OUT OF LEBANON

In September, marine artillery and the guns of the 6th Fleet were used to support Lebanese government troops against the rebels. America's ability to deter its enemies began to deteriorate in the following year. On October 23, 1983, terrorists driving trucks loaded with explosives penetrated the perimeter of the marine barracks in Beirut. The blasts killed 241 U.S. Marines. It was widely assumed that Syria was behind the attack.

In early December, U.S. aircraft attacked Syrian antiaircraft positions in retaliation. The United States government considered doing more extensive damage to Syrian bases, but soon realized its options were limited. Reagan pulled the marines out of Lebanon in February 1984.

Before the disaster, an Israeli commentator had noted, "After much bloodshed among Lebanese, Syrians, Palestinians, and

President Ronald Reagan and First Lady Nancy Reagan pay their respects to the victims of an attack on U.S. barracks in Beirut during the Lebanese civil war. On October 23, 1983, a truck loaded with the equivalent of 12,000 pounds of TNT exploded and collapsed the four-story building, killing 241 American servicemen. Two minutes later the eight-story Drakkar barracks were leveled, killing 58 French soldiers.

Israelis, the United States, without firing a shot, became the dominant power in an area previously ruled by two close allies of the Soviet Union." The United States no longer wanted to accept that role. It had suffered too much, and the American public did not want to see any more body bags coming home.

Three minutes after the last marine left the beach in Beirut on February 26, the U.S. seashore base was taken over by gunmen of the Shia Muslim Amal movement, which was linked to Syria and Iran. Some of the gunmen had little pictures of the Iranian religious leader, Ayatollah Khomeini, around their necks.

The Israelis were satisfied that they had expelled the PLO from Beirut and saw no reason for further conflict. They pulled back in 1985 to a security zone in southern Lebanon. The Syrians remained in parts of the country, and continued to exert their controlling interest in Lebanon. A sort of uneasy peace descended on the region.

10

The Strongman

The man who dominated Syria during this period and the next—indeed, who would run Syria longer than any other leader in modern history—was Hafez al-Assad. Born October 6, 1930, in the farming community of Qardaha, a mud and stone dwellings, Assad was a quiet, gangly boy who showed an early interest in politics. He hated the French, who then occupied Syria, and developed an early interest in Arab nationalism. He was a member of the Alawi sect of Shiites in a country where Sunnis were in the majority.

Assad was fortunate; his father was one of the few literate people in the village and encouraged his son's studies. Hafez was elected president of the Union of Syrian Students and attended the Syrian Military Academy. After graduation, he joined the elite air force and became a fighter pilot. He was named the best pilot in his class at an air training school in Aleppo. His experience as a pilot gave him a lifelong appreciation of the importance of aircraft in combat.

ASSAD RISES IN POWER

Assad opposed Syria's union with Egypt in the United Arab Republic. He supported pan-Arabism, but felt that the UAR gave Nasser too much power. He was able to form a military committee of Syrian officers serving in Egypt, and in 1963 the committee helped bring the Ba'ath Party into power in a bloodless coup d'état. Assad held the rank of major general and was named air force commander. After another coup in 1966, he was named defense minister. In 1970, still another coup elevated him to prime minister. He was elected president for a seven-year term in 1971 and was regularly and easily reelected after that. The magazine *The Economist* once called the Syrian government under Assad "a family and tribal clique within a military junta." (A junta is a group of people who get together to run a country, usually following a revolution.)

Assad was a soft-spoken man with a high forehead and small mustache. As an observant Muslim, he neither drank alcohol nor smoked, and did not eat meat. He was also a workaholic, spending long hours doing government work, and had practically no social life. Assad's great hero was the Kurdish warrior Salah al-Din, known as Saladin, who defeated the Crusaders. Assad had a picture of Saladin on his office wall.

Assad made strong efforts to rebuild his economically depressed country and rid the government of long-entrenched corruption. He built roads, schools, hospitals, and low-cost housing. But the major goal of his life was to take revenge on the Israelis for Syria's humiliating defeat in the 1967 Six-Day War.

ASSAD FIGHTS TO RECLAIM THE GOLAN HEIGHTS

Assad was particularly passionate about reclaiming the Golan Heights. He saw Israeli occupation of the strategically and symbolically important high ground as a dagger aimed at Syria's heart. This passion colored all of his dealings with Israel and hindered any chance of a peace treaty with the hated enemy.

In the 1973 Yom Kippur War, Assad managed to reclaim a slice of territory in Golan. In later peace talks with Kissinger, he managed to retain another part as well. The amount of territory was insignificant from a strategic point of view. Nevertheless, Assad saw these gains as a victory.

After the Soviet Union's demise in 1991, Syria no longer had the backing of its old ally. So, Assad reluctantly entered into negotiations with Israel on a possible peace treaty. These talks were held in conjunction with the administration of then-U.S.

Hafez al-Assad, president of Syria, shakes the hand of Bill Clinton, president of the United States, during a meeting to discuss a peace treaty between Syria and Israel.

president Bill Clinton. However, the talks did not get very far, primarily because of Assad's determination to make the return of the Golan Heights a requirement for peace.

Assad died on June 10, 2000, after nearly three decades of rule, and Syria moved into a new phase of its history. This phase was dependent on Assad's son, Bashar, who succeeded him.

BASHAR AL-ASSAD BECOMES PRESIDENT

Bashar al-Assad began his regime by vowing to reform an economy saddled with archaic laws, backward technology, a stifling bureaucracy, and rampant corruption. He approved new laws to establish private banks, and introduced measures to set up a stock market and private universities and to liberalize the currency system. *The Washington Post*, in an article on March 27, 2001, used the example of a state-owned cookie factory in Damascus to illustrate what Bashar faced in trying to change the Syrian economy:

> [A]t the Ghraoui Biscuit Co., 90 workers churn out their notoriously unpopular tea biscuits, even though the plant's market has dwindled to a few state-owned stores, the workweek has shrunk to four days, and Syrian officials say a portion of the goods go home with the employees.

In most capitalist societies, the plant would have been put out of business long ago. Still, closing it would have been virtually impossible in Syria. Syrians believe the system that keeps such unprofitable and inefficient businesses going is crucial to social harmony. Keeping it open, however, meant giving in to a system that had corroded the country's economy and elevated corruption and cronyism to the normal way of conducting business.

Bashar was handed a country that his father had allowed to drift toward obsolescence. How could he create a private banking system where there were no bankers? How could he install modern management without trained managers, and how could he shed assets like the crumbling cookie factory without alienating the political allies he needed to stay in power?

Some things had not changed in a Syria used to firm control from the top. One day in 2001, a man named Nizar Nayyouf was yanked out of his car in broad daylight by police, who threw a sack over his head and whisked him away.

Apparently, security forces had acted on their own, as they were accustomed to doing. Only an order from the top secured

Nayyouf's release. The government then tried to say the abduction had never taken place.

Actually, the fact that Nayyouf, whose "crime" was not revealed, survived the abduction without being tortured or killed, a frequent occurrence in the Hafez al-Assad era, indicated that things might be less repressive under Bashar. Yet, Bashar continued his father's policy of blasting Israel. In March 2001, he said Israeli society is "more racist than the Nazis."

When Pope John Paul II arrived in Damascus in May 2001, he found himself standing silently by as Bashar launched into a tirade against the Jews, calling them betrayers of Jesus. Asked why the pope had not responded to the Syrian, all the Vatican could say was that the pope and the Catholic Church are strongly opposed to anti-Semitism.

Then in January 2002, Syria's deputy United Nations ambassador, Fayssal Mekdad, used the occasion of Syria's first speech as a new member of the UN Security Council to accuse Israel of "state terrorism" against the Palestinians. He compared recent Israeli actions against Palestinians in the Rafah refugee camp in Gaza, where Israeli tanks demolished houses of suspected terrorists, to the devastation of the World Trade Center on September 11, 2001. The United States responded by calling the statement "extremely unfortunate, unhelpful, and offensive."

It was unlikely that Mekdad made his remarks without clearance from Bashar al-Assad. This led to speculation that, as much as Assad wanted to make changes in his country, he still had to appease those who wanted to continue the hard line against Israel. For example, the issue of terrorism and Syria's role in fostering or combating it has become a significant issue for the new regime.

The story of Khalid al-Shami helps to illustrate this point. Al-Shami had spent 20 years in prison for being a ranking member of the Muslim Brotherhood, a fundamentalist Islamic movement. Now, with Bashar in control, al-Shami was released from prison in December 2001, but found himself lost in a Damascus he did not recognize. "I couldn't find my house because every-thing had changed," he told a *New York Times* reporter. "I didn't know where I was."

SYRIA SUSPECTED OF TERRORISM

The Muslim Brotherhood was only one of the groups suppressed during Hafez al-Assad's years of rule. He had been severely criti-cized by Amnesty International and other groups for his record of civil rights violations. Furthermore, because of its anti-Israeli role, Syria had been on the United States' list of countries that sup-ported terrorists since 1979. The U.S. State Department claimed Syria provided the terrorist organization of Abu Nidal with logis-tical support and permission to operate facilities in Damascus. (Abu Nidal was a Palestinian who founded the terrorist group Fatah, and was for a time considered the most dangerous terrorist in the world.) Reports in the 1980s said Syria provided training camps for Middle Eastern and international terrorists. There were five training bases near Damascus and some 20 other training facilities elsewhere in the country, according to the reports.

U.S. News & World Report wrote in 1986 that large numbers of international terrorists known to Western intelligence agen-cies had turned up in Damascus in the early 1980s. Even West-ern European terrorists were reported to have trained in Syria and Lebanon. They included such unrelated groups as the Red Army Faction, also known as the Baader-Meinhof Gang, of Ger-many; the Armenian Secret Army for the Liberation of Armenia; the Japanese Red Army; the Kurdish Labor Party; the Pakistani Az Zulifkar; and the Tamil United Liberation Front, as well as groups from Sri Lanka, the Philippines, Oman, Somalia, and other countries.

Middle East analysts found that Syrian intelligence services used terrorist organizations to further the country's interests and to eliminate opposition. The Syrians also used terrorists as surrogates to avoid direct blame, analysts said. Some operated outside the country.

Jordanian officials accused Syria of being behind the assassination of two Jordanian diplomats in Athens and Madrid, and of wounding two others in India and Italy. PLO leaders accused Syria of the assassination of Said Sayil, also known as Abu Walid, Yasir Arafat's chief of staff.

In the U.S. Department of State's *Patterns of Global Terrorism: 1983*, it was reported that several attacks by members of the Abu Nidal organization were traced to Syrian opposition to the pro-Arafat Fatah faction of the PLO.

The attacks included the murder of Issam Sartqwi, a PLO observer at the International Conference of Socialists in Portugal. The same report charged Syria with encouraging the radical Shia Lebanese group Islamic Jihad to carry out the 1983 suicide bombing attacks against the U.S. Embassy and the marine barracks in Beirut.

Spotted in Damascus were Abu Musa, leader of a radical PLO faction who had nearly succeeded in taking the Palestinian leadership from Yasir Arafat, and Habib Shartouni, who was said to have admitted killing Lebanese President Bashir Gemayel in 1982, touching off the Syrian invasion of Lebanon.

ASSAD WORKS WITH THE WEST

In 1987, Assad closed Abu Nidal's office in Damascus and worked to win the release of French and U.S. hostages held by terrorist groups. In that year, also, Assad resumed normal diplomatic relations with the United States.

In 1990, when Iraq suddenly invaded Kuwait, President George H. W. Bush rounded up a number of other countries, including Arab nations, to help defeat Iraqi dictator Saddam Hussein. Assad was glad to help and contributed an armored division to the multinational "Desert Storm" force that liberated Kuwait.

That sent his stock up with Western countries. So, during that time, he had taken advantage of the world's focus on the Persian Gulf to move the Syrian army deeper into Lebanon and install a pro-Syrian president in Beirut, or so the Lebanese

Former American hostage Edward Austin Tracy *(left)* addresses the media under a portrait of Hafez al-Assad during a press conference at the Syrian Foreign Ministry in August 1991. Tracy was kidnapped in Beirut, Lebanon, in October 1986 by the Islamic militant group Organization of Revolutionary Justice (ORJ) and held for five years.

nationalists contended. The Israelis finally evacuated Lebanon in May 2000, leaving the country to Syria, which installed a pro-Syrian government.

Assad was not ready to give up his demand that Israel return what he considered to be Syrian property. In an interview with the *Washington Post*, Assad declared, "If Israel is not going to quit the occupied land, why then should we want peace? No people can accept anything as a substitute for their land."

Even President Bill Clinton was not able to change Assad's mind. The two met in Geneva—a significant and often-criticized move—in March 2000, but Assad continued to insist that without the return of the Golan Heights, there would be no peace treaty with Israel.

THE GOLAN HEIGHTS

The Golan Heights is a 40-mile-long, 12-mile-wide, boat-shaped strategic high ground that had been the central issue blocking a peace settlement between Israel and Syria since 1967.

That was when Israel took the Golan Heights from Syria in the Six-Day War. Israel was determined to hang on to the territory; Syria was just as determined to win it back. Hafez al-Assad refused to do more than devote rhetoric to negotiating a treaty with Israel as long as Israel held on to the Golan Heights.

Standing on the Golan Heights, a visitor can see the flat expanse of land that separates the promontory from Damascus, 40 miles away. Israel feared that if the ground was returned to Syria, the Syrians might use it to shell Israeli settlements, as they had done in the past. Syria was just as fearful that the Israelis would use the Golan as a jumping off point to invade Syria.

The Israelis made the Golan fruitful during their occupation. They grew fruits and vegetables among the rugged hills, including grapes for a highly praised wine. Where Syrian guns once pointed at Israel, cattle and sheep grazed. About 15,000 people established 32 settlements on the fertile land.

Above, Israeli Druze women harvest grapes for the Golan Heights Winery in Moshav Odem on the Golan Heights. Founded 23 years ago on the volcanic plateau that Israel captured from Syria in the 1967 Six-Day War, the winery produces award-winning wines.

On the southern end, the farmers cultivated plums, apricots, nectarines, mangoes, grapefruit, bananas, dates, and avocados. On the northern end, blueberry fields and orchards of apples, pears, peaches, and cherries thrived. The farmers also grew cotton, corn, tomatoes, and onions. Dairy cattle dined on the lush grasses.

Manufacturing plants, producing many products—from machinery to film to food packaging to tiles, wall coverings, shoes, and many other goods—were also built on the Golan Heights.

Before the terrorist bombings and killings in the continuing struggle between the Israelis and Palestinians intensified, the Israelis promoted the Golan Heights as a tourist attraction. Visitors enjoyed spectacular scenery, waterfalls, and snow. The Golan Heights was the only area under Israeli control where snow could be found. Mount Hermon on the northern end is 9,232 feet high and offered a year-round chairlift for skiers.

The Golan Heights is also the site of the Crusader fortress of Ka'alat Namrud and a number of archaeological sites.

Another reason why the Israelis wanted to hang on to the heights was water. When Syria had occupied the territory, it had earlier tried to dry out the Jewish state by diverting the sources of the Jordan River, when Israel began its National Water Carrier project in 1963. Israelis say that whoever occupies the region controls a third of Israel's water supply.

In a dry and thirsty land, that is important, even crucial.

Under the administration of Israeli Prime Minister Ehud Barak, the Israeli government talked about the possibility of vacating the Golan Heights, except for a narrow strip along the Sea of Galilee.

When President Clinton presented this offer to Hafez al-Assad, the Syrian leader rejected it out of hand. "That is the place I know as the border between Israel and Syria," he told the president. "Up until 1967, I would swim in the Sea of Galilee. I would have barbecues. I ate fish."

Two new presidents, George W. Bush of the United States and Hafez's son Bashar, were the inheritors of the seemingly impossible standoff over the Golan Heights. They would have their turn at trying to make a breakthrough.

WORKING TOWARD BETTER RELATIONS WITH THE UNITED STATES

Meanwhile, a strong indication that Bashar al-Assad wanted better relations with the United States came in an interview with the Knight Ridder News Service in June 2002. In that interview he discussed how, just a few months earlier, Syria had provided intelligence to the United States about Osama bin Laden's al Qaeda terrorist network, which was responsible for the attacks on the United States that occurred on September 11, 2001.

Assad said information his country provided to the United States three months earlier had saved the lives of American soldiers who would have been the victims of yet another terrorist attack. Although he declined to give specifics, he said that if the terrorist operation had been successful, it would have killed many American soldiers. Assad hoped to deflect some of the criticism that his country harbored terrorists. In articles published by Knight Ridder–owned newspapers on June 19, 2002, he complained that despite his cooperation, Syria continued to be identified by the United States as a country that sponsors terrorism. He said his aim was to get his country off that list.

A U.S. intelligence official confirmed that Syria had cooperated in U.S. antiterrorist efforts, but declined to provide details. "The Syrians have been cooperative and supportive in the fight against al-Qaeda, including providing useful information and providing threat information," the official was quoted as saying.

Another intelligence official confirmed that Mohammed Haydar Zammar, a German citizen born in Syria, who helped recruit Mohamed Atta and other September 11 airplane hijackers in Hamburg, was in Syrian custody. There were indications that Syrian authorities may have allowed U.S. intelligence agents to question Zammar about his activities. There was also evidence that the United States has sent terrorism suspects to Syria to be tortured.

These and other events seemed to indicate Syria's willingness to help the United States crack down on terrorists. There was hope that this willingness might lead to Syria's removal from the list of countries sponsoring terrorism and mark the beginning for that country to play a role in the struggle for peace in the Middle East. However, many observers felt that Syria's actual motives at this time may have been different, perhaps because al Qaeda threatened the Syrian regime.

Syria in Recent Years

Despite the high hopes of many, recent years in Syria have been volatile and uncertain. Bashar al-Assad's assumption of the presidency, following his father's thirty years in power, had brought hope to many Syrians of significant reforms and improvements in the country's economic development, its relationships with other countries, and its domestic affairs. Still, Assad's administration has been able to fulfill these hopes only partially. Peace and prosperity in Syria, as in the Middle East as a whole, have remained elusive.

THE DAMASCUS SPRING

Still, the first years of the twenty-first century were, for Syria, marked by at least the prospect of change. On the heels of the transfer of power, a period of reform known as the Damascus Spring emerged. This period lasted from the summer of 2000 to the autumn of 2001, roughly coinciding with the first year of the younger Assad's administration. The purposes of the Damascus Spring were foreshadowed in the new president's inaugural address when he stated his intention to create, among other things, a more open government. "There is no doubt," he said, "that transparency is an important thing."

More Freedom

There were a number of gradually increasing freedoms for Syria during the Damascus Spring. For example, censorship was relaxed and newspapers, magazines, and other media were allowed greater independence. Also, many reform-minded Syrians were allowed to organize discussion groups known as salons, and the use of the Internet was allowed. Salons and online discussion groups were sources of intense debate on such subjects as free speech, the rights of women, and the creation of multiple political parties.

Another aspect of the gradual freedoms of the Damascus Spring involved a series of highly visible and well-publicized demonstrations. These rallies took place all around Syria, but primarily in the capital city. They reflected a wide array of dissident issues, including the need for a faster pace of political and

Young Syrians wave flags in al-Rawda Square near the U.S. embassy during a sit-in in Damascus in 2005. Syrian president Bashar al-Assad freed 190 political prisoners as part of an effort for overall reforms.

economic reform in Syria, the release of political detainees, an end to martial law, the establishment of a completely free press, and a relaxation of restrictions on public debate.

To an extent, the new president tried to pay heed to the concerns voiced in these demonstrations. For example, Assad released some political prisoners. He also shook up the top levels of Syria's armed forces and security services by making it mandatory for military officers to retire at age 60. This replaced a number of long-entrenched commanders with younger officers.

Decrease in Corruption

At the same time, the new president moved to curb the increasingly blatant corruption and incompetence in Syria's civilian administration. For example, the director-general of the state-run Commercial Bank of Syria was arrested after losing some $5 million in bad investments. The head of the state-run Syrian Airlines was just one of dozens of other officials and bureaucrats who were dismissed or arrested for mismanagement or misconduct. The Syrian government's record of negligence and corruption became especially obvious in the wake of a serious disaster in June 2002, when a structurally defective and overloaded dam on the Orontes River (built only six years earlier) collapsed, causing floods and numerous deaths.

Political Reform

More evidence of Damascus's slowly opening stance toward reform was seen in March 2003, when elections were held for Syria's parliament, the 250-member People's Assembly. One hundred and seventy-eight new members were elected. The vast majority of these were members of the dominant Ba'ath Party. Among the new members were also four representatives of the Syrian Social Nationalist Party, a longtime rival of the Ba'ath Party, as well as seven independents. Furthermore, many of the new delegates were relatively young—under the age of 50.

Global Relations

Meanwhile, Syria was working to improve its relations with other countries. The country took a significant step in foreign affairs in 2002, when it won a seat as the only Arab nation on the UN Security Council despite the strenuous objections of Israel and several other countries. During its two-year term, Syria had limited powers—it was not allowed to vote on the council's decisions—but it was privy to the council's deliberations, including delicate discussions on antiterrorism.

The U.S.-led invasion of neighboring Iraq in 2003 had a profound effect on Syria. The conflict affected many aspects of the country's foreign relations, economy, and domestic affairs. To cite one example, the invasion of Iraq created a major dilemma for Syria, as hundreds of thousands of refugees began pouring into the country from Iraq. While Syria welcomed these refugees as guests, who now number more than 1.5 million, Damascus increasingly found it difficult to provide basic services such as health care and education for them.

The war also upset Syria's commercial trade with Iraq. Syrian companies that had enjoyed a favored market there for a wide range of consumer goods were suddenly deprived of those markets. The most crucial aspect of this was a halt to oil transportation.

Some 200,000 barrels a day of Iraqi crude oil had once flowed from Iraq to the Mediterranean port of Banyas, Syria (most of which was then transported elsewhere). This arrangement had allowed Syria to charge lucrative transport fees; when these stopped, Syria's economy suffered badly.

Furthermore, the war in Iraq had a profound impact on Syria's foreign relations. During the first Gulf War, in 1991, Damascus had briefly aligned itself with the United States against Iraqi strongman Saddam Hussein. In 2003, however, Syria vehemently opposed the U.S.-led military operations against Saddam, considering it a pro-Israeli blow against Arab nations as a whole. (Arabs had generally viewed Saddam as the leader most likely to oppose Israel.) A number of prominent Syrian leaders publicly denounced the invasion.

For example, Vice President Abd al-Halim Khaddam stated, "The American attack against Iraq is designed to bring about the partition of that country, which serves as a strategic target for Israel, and is in fact part of a longtime Zionist plan to break up the fabric of national unity of the countries in the region." Syria's minister of information, Adnan Umran, added, "Involvement of Americans in the domestic affairs of the Arab countries is reminiscent of the colonial period, and if Washington could, it would bring us all back to that period." President Assad himself stated that the United States was "interested only in gaining control over Iraqi oil and redrawing the map of the region in keeping with its worldview."

As might be expected, the official U.S. response to these comments was equally strong. American officials repeatedly charged that Syria was allowing troops and military supplies to cross into Iraq to support Saddam Hussein. They also charged that Syria was secretly but actively aiding terrorist organizations (including Hezbollah, Hamas, and Palestinian Islamic Jihad) both within and outside its borders. Syrian government spokesmen vigorously denied these charges, but Washington rebuffed them, alleging that most of the anti-Coalition troops captured in Iraq were from Syria and Lebanon—or had at least passed through Syria from elsewhere.

U.S.-Syrian relations continued to deteriorate, and Syria's economy was dealt a further (if largely symbolic) blow when U.S. President George W. Bush signed a bill imposing strict economic sanctions against the Arab nation. These sanctions included an embargo on most trade and a ban on transactions with Syria's commercial banking.

The reasons given for the sanctions were numerous, including Syria's support of terrorism, its ongoing occupation of Lebanon, its development of weapons of mass destruction, and its trade with Iraq. However, some commentators have pointed out that these sanctions were more of a political statement than an actual

Brigadier General Elhadji Mouhamadou Kandji of Senegal, head of a nine-member UN team charged with verifying Syria's troop withdrawal from Lebanon, inspects a former Syrian military post in Rayak.

blow to Syria's economy, since U.S.-Syrian trade and U.S. investment in Syria was relatively small.

During this period, the United States maintained a policy of closely monitoring Syrian military activities. Notably, U.S. forces in Iraq moved to the Syrian border in the summer of 2004, monitoring events across the frontier with unmanned drone aircraft. American officials also persuaded the UN Security Council to pass a resolution demanding the withdrawal of Syria's military presence from Lebanon and the disarming of Lebanese militias. Syrian military camps around Beirut were removed in September, and Syria's foreign minister, Farouk al-Shara, met his U.S. counterpart, Secretary of State Colin Powell, at the United Nations to discuss the situation.

END OF THE DAMASCUS SPRING

Meanwhile, in terms of Syria's ongoing attempts at domestic reforms, the hopes raised by the Damascus Spring movement were fading. When it became clear that the United States would enter Iraq, a number of Syria's newly won freedoms were crushed. In many cases, this was apparently because Assad feared for his regime's stability—or perhaps feared an invasion of his own country.

For example, the tentative beginnings of free speech in Syria quickly came to an end. Assad, worried that anti-Arab forces threatened the country, cracked down by closing magazines and jailing journalists and activists. This crackdown was perhaps typified by the fate of the country's only private newspaper, the outspoken *Al Domari*, which shut down in 2003 after a long period of government harassment and criticism. The newspaper had been forced to close down briefly several times in the past; this time, its license was permanently revoked.

Still, the spirit of reform lived on in some ways. Early in 2004, for instance, about 1,000 prominent Syrian intellectuals signed a petition urging a number of immediate reforms, including an end to martial law, the release of dissident prisoners, and amnesty for exiled activists.

Such calls came in the midst of frequent, distracting out-bursts of ethnic violence. For example, in the spring of 2004, violence broke out at a football (soccer) match in the Kurdish town of Al-Qamishli in northeast Syria. Reports indicated that it started when Kurdish spectators brandished a Kurdish flag and pictures of George W. Bush, whom they supported. Confronting them were fans chanting slogans and waving banners in support of Saddam Hussein. When police shot into the crowd, a dozen Kurds died. This incident then blossomed into widespread rioting, looting, the burning of buildings, and arrests throughout Syria's Kurdish communities.

The deadly violence continued through the year, including an incident in which a dozen bombs detonated simultaneously in Damascus. Reform activists, including a number of presidential advisers, publicly stated that the situation was intolerable. In June, Assad announced that he would try again to institute reforms. He installed new people in several high-level positions, including Syria's defense and interior ministries. Such moves, however, did not relax the government's overall grip on civil rights, including a ban on political activities by unlicensed organizations.

SYRIA'S RELATIONS WITH LEBANON

Syria's domination of Lebanese affairs continued to be a sore point for many nations. A shocking event early in 2005 kept this volatile situation in the spotlight. On February 14, Rafiq al-Hariri was assassinated, along with 21 others, by a car bomb that destroyed his motorcade in Beirut. Hariri was a former two-time prime minister of Lebanon and a popular, independent politician who had been outspoken in his opposition to Syria's involvement in his country.

Damascus publicly condemned the assassination. Nonetheless, a number of nations, including Lebanon and the United States, strongly stated their suspicions that Syrian intelligence forces were complicit in it.

The assassination polarized factions within Lebanon and triggered a widespread, grassroots anti-Syrian movement that became known as the Cedar Revolution (also called the February 14 movement). The day after the explosion, the Ba'ath Party office in Beirut was attacked by an angry mob. At the end of February, a huge crowd, estimated at 25,000, demonstrated at Hariri's grave site. Many other public demonstrations and out-pourings of popular feeling bolstered outrage over the death.

The assassination was also condemned internationally. President Bush renewed his demand that Syria remove its forces from

Lebanon. The European Union and the UN, with Security Council Resolution 1559, also strongly supported this position. At first, Syria responded by simply shifting its troops, moving them to the eastern edge of the Al-Biqa' valley in central Lebanon. Then, in late March, Foreign Minister Farouk al-Shara promised the UN that Syria's forces would leave Lebanon completely before that country's parliamentary elections in May.

Syria made good on this promise. The last Syrian soldiers left Lebanese territory on April 26, 2005. This move ended Syria's twenty-nine-year-long occupation of its neighbor.

In the wake of this landmark event, Damascus and Beirut resumed their stalled discussions over various issues, including ongoing border disputes and the question of supplying Syrian natural gas to Lebanese electrical plants. Nonetheless, tensions remained high between the two nations. For example, Syrian guards harassed Lebanese commercial vehicles crossing the border. Lebanese police carried out raids against suspected smugglers in border districts. Syrian patrol boats seized Lebanese fishing vessels in contested waters.

After Hariri's death, a special UN commission, headed by a distinguished German prosecutor, Detlev Mehlis, had been created to conduct an investigation into it. Mehlis and his 100-strong team of investigators spent months sifting evidence and interviewing hundreds of people. The United States, Great Britain, and France also sponsored a Security Council resolution demanding full Syrian cooperation with the Hariri investigation.

The Mehlis report, released in October 2005, surprised both the Lebanese and Syrian political establishments by directly implicating a number of pro-Syrian security chiefs and officials in Lebanon who had since resigned. At a press conference, Mehlis firmly stated, "They [the pro-Syrian security heads] participated to some extent in the planning that led to the assassination of Hariri." A further investigation found that Syrian intelligence agents were still active in Lebanese affairs, despite the ostensible end of Syrian involvement in that country. The Hariri assassination caused a major shake-up in Damascus. President Assad

On the left is the three-story building housing the embassies of Chile, Sweden, and Denmark in Damascus after Syrian demonstrators set it ablaze following the publication of cartoons depicting the Prophet Muhammad negatively in Danish newspapers. The Norwegian embassy was also set on fire. Fortunately, there were no injuries.

dismissed General Hasan Khalil as chief of military intelligence and appointed his brother-in-law, General Asaf Shawkat, in Khalil's place. Then, less than two weeks before the publication of the Mehlis report, Interior Minister Ghazi Kanaan was found dead, an apparent suicide. For twenty years, Kanaan had been the head of Syrian military intelligence in Lebanon. The death of Kanaan, a major witness, was a stunning development in the ongoing investigation. Marwan Hamade, the Lebanese minister of telecommunications and a close friend of the slain premier—as well as someone who narrowly missed an attempt on his own life—commented about Kanaan's death, "It's certainly related to the Hariri inquiry and absolutely will have an impact."

The Hariri assassination did nothing to improve Syria's relations with the United States, which were going from bad to worse. Damascus claimed to be renewing its efforts to reduce the flow of troops and supplies into Iraq, but officials in Washington dismissed these claims as having only the appearance of sincerity.

In February 2006, another international crisis developed. Syria was part of the worldwide furor that took place when a Danish newspaper published a cartoon depicting the Prophet Muhammad as a terrorist. (Images of the Prophet are typically banned under Islamic custom.) The cartoon sparked widespread violence across the Arab world, including marches and riots that burned the Danish, Norwegian, and French embassies in Damascus.

SYRIA STRENGTHENS FOREIGN TIES

Throughout the rest of 2006, Syria's relations with other countries remained problematic. In some cases, Damascus was able to strengthen its foreign ties. For example, its alliance with Iran was strengthened when Syria and Iran signed a mutual defense pact. The two countries also announced plans to jointly build an industrial complex outside the Syrian city of Homs, to be used as a base for various Iranian-funded technology projects.

Syria also strengthened its alliances with Russia during this period. Part of this effort involved the two countries' reaching an agreement to cooperate closely on Syrian nuclear power projects. It also involved reaching an agreement to let warships from the Russian Black Sea Fleet use two key Syrian ports, Latakia and Tartus. To protect these ships, antimissile batteries were planned for both ports.

Furthermore, Syria bolstered its ties with China, a rising world power. China has in recent years become Syria's biggest import partner, and Damascus has been conducting talks with Beijing aimed at creating still larger trade markets and higher levels of investment by the Chinese in Syria, especially in such areas as information technology, petrochemicals, agriculture, textiles, and energy.

In June 2007, the two countries signed a series of agreements that marked a significant step. They established economic cooperation between Syria and China and activated previous agreements concerning such issues as higher education, transport, and communications. This was obviously good for Syria, but it was also good for China because with it Syria officially recognized China's "market economy status." The Chinese government hopes that this recognition will strengthen Beijing's position as it increases its overall role in international trade.

MORE FIGHTING WITH LEBANON

On the other hand, some of Syria's foreign ties have not improved in recent years. Paramount among these has been its longstanding tensions with Israel. These have periodically burst into outright violence, notably a bloody-but-inconclusive conflict in the summer of 2006 between Israeli forces and Syria-backed Hezbollah along the border. The "July War" caused more than 1,200 deaths and made tens of thousands of Lebanese citizens into refugees. The conflict ended after 34 days when the UN passed a cease-fire resolution and sent a 13,000-member peacekeeping force from 30 countries to the region.

In 2006, there were new developments in the ongoing investigation into the Hariri assassination. Detlev Mehlis, the German prosecutor who had headed the investigation, returned to Bonn and was replaced by a Belgian-born prosecutor, Serge Brammertz. Meanwhile, Syrian intelligence agents were implicated in another prominent political murder in Lebanon. In the fall of 2006, Pierre Amine Gemayel, a young Lebanese cabinet minister who had been a strong critic of Syria's involvement in his country, was gunned down in a suburb of Beirut.

In the wake of Gemayel's assassination, fingers were pointed in several directions. Those suspected included political rivals of the Gemayel family within Lebanon, but Damascus was also suspected. No hard evidence has yet surfaced and no one has yet been directly accused. A *Washington Post* journalist, David Ignatius, noted at the time, "Given the brutal history of Syria's involvement in Lebanon, there's an instant temptation to blame Damascus. But in this land of death, there are so many killers and so few means of holding them to account that we can only guess at who pulled the trigger."

Ignatius added that, no matter who was to blame, the multiple incidents of violence—and the multiple failures of peaceful negotiation—were threatening to destroy all of the Arab countries. "A disease is eating away at the Middle East," he wrote. "It is the idea that the only political determinant in the Arab world is raw force—the power of physical intimidation. It is politics as assassination."

The ongoing investigation into the assassination of Hariri has, more recently, led to the formation in June 2007 of an international tribunal to try suspects in the crime. The announcement of the tribunal's formation sparked a fresh wave of bomb attacks in Beirut.

Some of these attacks were small and apparently random. One that was not random targeted a pro-Western Lebanese Parliament member, Walid Eido. Eido, his son, two bodyguards, and six passersby were killed, and a dozen more were wounded, when a bomb hidden inside a parked car exploded as Eido drove past.

Lebanon's pro-Western prime minister, Fouad Siniora, declared a national day of mourning in the wake of the crime and vowed that Lebanon would remain united. According to the *New York Times*, he stated, "Our determination to fight evil and betrayal will remain strong and effective." The speaker of the Lebanese Parliament, Nabih Berri, a close ally of Hezbollah, also condemned the attack. He said, "No individual, group, organization or party using terrorism and organized crime will be able to make Lebanon an arena for unrest, strife, wars and score-settling."

Eido's assassination was apparently designed to fracture Lebanese politics, upsetting the fragile coalition of Sunni Muslim,

Christian, and Druze politicians who oppose Syrian control of Lebanon and who found common ground after the assassination of Hariri, a Sunni. Although it is widely suspected that Syrian-backed forces were behind the killing, some observers speculate that the event may backfire on them. Writing in the *Wall Street Journal*, Middle East political scholar Joshua Muravchik notes, "Some feel that Eido's murder will solidify the majority in Lebanon's government that opposes Syria. They figure that trying to kill off the majority of members will only invite international intervention and fracture pro-Syrian forces."

As of mid-2007, it appears that Syria has not given up its interest in dominating affairs in Lebanon, since Damascus still sees that country as a crucial buffer between itself and Israel. The Cedar Revolution—the movement that had forced Syria to end its military occupation of Lebanon—appears to be unraveling. Furthermore, Emile Lahoud, who had served as the Lebanese president since 1998, was forced to resign in November 2007 without naming a successor, in part due to Syrian interference.

Since the Lebanese election in 2005 that narrowly voted in a majority led by Siniora, three anti-Syrian members of the Lebanese parliament, including Gemayel, have been murdered, and several more have resigned due to threats and intimidation. This has whittled Siniora's anti-Syria majority to only six seats. Lahoud and Parliamentary Speaker Nabih Berri, who are both sympathetic to Syria, refused to allow elections that would replace the murdered men.

The international community does not appear to be eager to confront Syria actively over its apparent continued involvement in Lebanon. This community was not jolted out of its passivity even by a car bomb that killed six UN peacekeepers in southern Lebanon in June 2007—the first attack on the United Nations Interim Force in Lebanon (UNIFIL) since it had been expanded after the 2006 war between Israel and Hezbollah.

Syria condemned the UNIFIL bombing, and Hezbollah has not so far been openly hostile to UNIFIL's presence in Lebanon. Furthermore, no evidence of Syria's involvement had been found as of mid-2007. Nonetheless, it has been widely suspected that Syrian forces had a hand in the attack. Those who suspect Damascus say that the attack may have been another warning to the UN to drop the tribunal that was investigating the Hariri assassination.

Throughout it all, Syria has continued to bear the criticism of other countries. For example, in June 2007, a scathing report by five independent experts for the UN Security Council found that Lebanon's border security was unable to prevent the ongoing smuggling of arms from Syria. Syria's record of human rights violations has also been criticized. In June of 2007, President Bush, hoping to weaken the Syrian regime, criticized Damascus for repressing freedom and held out hope to those Syrians who "yearn" for it. According to the *Washington Post*, Bush told them, "You are not bound forever by your misery. You plead in silence no longer. The free world hears you. You are not alone. America offers you its hand in friendship."

The United States and other nations are increasing pressure on Syria, fearing that Damascus may try to openly reenter Lebanon's affairs, setting up a parallel government in Beirut and arming Hezbollah and other militant groups. In July 2007, UN Secretary-General Ban Ki-moon expressed his dismay over this situation. He wrote in a report, "I am deeply concerned that Lebanon remains in the midst of a debilitating political crisis and faces ongoing attacks aimed at destabilizing and undermining its sovereignty."

EFFORTS TOWARD PEACE WITH ISRAEL

Intimately connected to the overall situation in Lebanon is the long-sought possibility of peace negotiations with Israel. These negotiations continue to be in flux. Talks between Israel and Syria had started, failed, and been restarted for years, typically with one side making the first move and the other refusing because it was not seen as a sincere effort. As of mid-2007, this situation had not changed. In June 2007, *Los Angeles Times* journalist Ken Ellingwood noted: "For months, Israel and Syria have sent signals that have alternated between bellicose and calming, leaving Israelis to speculate about the possibility of another summertime war and debate the merits of renewing negotiations with Damascus after a lull of seven years."

Bashar al-Assad has made public overtures since the inconclusive 2006 war, presumably with an eye toward regaining the Golan Heights, but Israeli Prime Minister Ehud Olmert has consistently questioned the Syrian leader's commitment to peace. He says that he feels that Assad wants peace not for the sake of peace, but only to improve Syrian relations with the United States. Olmert's spokeswoman, Miri Eisin, has stated, "The prime minister has always said he wants peace with Syria but doesn't think that the present Syrian government wants peace, but rather wants the peace process. It's always being evaluated." In a poll published in the summer of 2007 in the Israeli daily newspaper *Maariv*, there were indications that Israeli citizens agree; nearly three-fourths of those questioned said they did not believe Assad wants peace.

On their side, Syrian officials have said that they are willing to talk, but have also expressed doubt that Olmert's government is stable enough to make a deal. As of June 2007, Israel and Syria were tentatively considering renewing talks. However, it is unclear how they might reach an agreement even to sit down together at a negotiating table.

In the meantime, the current Syrian Foreign Minister, Walid Muallem, has said that his country is "more than ready" for talks, adding, "If the Israelis decide to renew the negotiations, they will find a willing partner." On the other hand, Syria's Vice President, Farouk al-Shara, has stated that renewed talks are unlikely because they do not have U.S. backing. He said, "We are not optimistic. The American president does not want peace between Israel and Syria."

Bush, for his part, has made clear his intention to let Syria and Israel conduct their own talks with no help from him. His administration hopes that continued sanctions will put so much pressure on Syria that it will be forced to make a peace deal with Israel. Richard N. Haass, president of the Council on Foreign Relations, wrote in 2007, "Syria is in a position to affect the movement of fighters into Iraq and arms into Lebanon. It also exercises considerable influence over Hamas. There is a strong case for working to get Syria to close its borders in exchange for economic benefits (provided by Arab governments, Europe and the United States) and a commitment to restart talks aimed at resolving the status of the Golan Heights. History shows that Syria…might be open to such a deal."

SYRIA LOOKS AHEAD

Despite all of the conflict and anguish caused by its multiple, overlapping problems, there is hope for Syria in the future. Much about the Syrian government and bureaucracy is still corrupt and authoritarian, but the seeds for change are there. For example, the Syrian constitution, adopted in 1973, guarantees such basic civil rights as free speech and assembly and freedom of the press (rights that have not been upheld).

Furthermore, there are encouraging signs in Bashar al-Assad's relative youth and his strong personal interest in Internet technology and other Western innovations—innovations with tremendous potential to open his country to outside influences. (Furthermore, Assad was trained in England and began his medical practice there.) Journalist Guy Taylor writes, "The young president seems to dance a tight rope between appeasing hardline allies of his father in Syria's vast security apparatus and permitting technology such as the World Wide Web to undermine the government's control of speech and opinion."

As with any country, building and maintaining a vibrant economy is a prime concern for the future in Syria. For the coming years, Damascus has committed itself to creating a mixed economy that will give greater scope to both the private sector and international investors. It will be important to make sure that ordinary Syrians who are not businesspeople can still make ends meet, so government employment and subsidies will most likely remain high. Dr. James Reilly, a Syria expert in the Department of Near and Middle Eastern Civilizations at the University of Toronto, notes: "For Syrians considering the issues facing their own country from their own perspectives and addressing their own priorities, the biggest issue in the coming years (unless they face a catastrophic foreign invasion) will be economic reform and subsistence guarantees."

Bashar al-Assad has so far succeeded with at least some of the delicate balancing required to solve these problems. For example, he has helped Syria undergo a significant transition from

Above, Syrians use the Internet at an Internet café in Damascus. Although Syrian officials boast a state-of-the-art press center with fast Internet access and wireless technology, the Syrian government is regulating the use of the Internet by its citizens, with writers and bloggers deemed harmful to state security facing the possibility of arrest.

a mostly state-run economy to one that includes a free market, while avoiding social unrest over economics; in other words, he has not triggered "bread riots" over food shortages.

Another serious problem that the administration in Damascus will face in the ongoing years is the enormous influx of refugees fleeing in the wake of the 2003 U.S.-Iraqi war. An estimated 1.5 million Iraqis have fled their country and are living in Syria, with some 20,000 to 30,000 more still arriving every month. Both the general population and the government of Syria have been understanding of the situation, and they have welcomed these refugees in the name of Arab solidarity. Nonetheless, the huge influx has created a significant strain on Syria's already taxed infrastructures and services. Finding housing, jobs, and education for these refugees is a massive challenge.

Syria has tried to cope. For example, the country has put its schools on double shifts to handle the huge numbers of new students, but it lacks the capacity to adequately handle education for all of the Iraqi children who have become refugees there. Ron Redmond, a spokesman for the United Nations High Commissioner for Refugees (UNHCR), said in July 2007, "A whole generation of Iraqi children is in danger of missing out on an education."

Whatever happens with this and other issues, the history of Syria in recent years has been, and will be, inextricably interwoven with the life of one man—Bashar al-Assad. (This has been a recurrent problem in Syria and, indeed, most Arab countries.) Many observers agree that he has done well in some respects in moving his country toward a free market economy while still maintaining social peace. On the other hand, in the eyes of many, Assad has failed in other respects. For example, although he has proved less authoritarian than his father, he has been slow to grant the civil freedoms he originally promised. Middle East scholar Eyal Zisser notes, "Some believe that the apple hasn't fallen far from the tree and that Bashar is essentially a loyal follower in his father's footsteps, personality differences, and changed circumstances notwithstanding. By contrast, others point out that he is, after all, a young man with an open mind and especially with a deep acquaintance with the West."

In May 2007, Bashar al-Assad was elected to a second seven-year term as president of Syria. Time will tell which aspect of Assad—and which fate for his country—will prevail.

Chronology

1516	Ottoman Turks add Syria to their empire.
1916–1918	Syrians and other Arabs revolt against Turks.
1916	Sykes-Picot Agreement; Great Britain and France divide up Middle East.
1917	Balfour Declaration promises British support for a Jewish homeland in Palestine.
1918	T.E. Lawrence and British troops march into Damascus.
1920	France receives Syria as a League of Nations mandate.
1936	First Syrian national government established under French.

Timeline

1946
Syria becomes independent country when French pull out

1916
Sykes-Picot Agreement; Great Britain and France divide up Middle East

1949
Military overthrows Syrian government; first of many coups

1970
Hafez al-Assad becomes president

1916 · · · · · **1973**

1936
First Syrian national government established under French

1967
Israel defeats Syria, Egypt, and Jordan in Six-Day War; Israel takes Golan Heights from Syria

1973
Syria and Egypt attack Israel on Yom Kippur; U.S. secretary of state Henry Kissinger conducts shuttle diplomacy between Syria and Israel

1940	Germany conquers France, sets up Vichy government.
1944	United States and Soviet Union recognize Syria and Lebanon as sovereign states.
1945	French bombard Damascus to quash uprising.
1946	Syria becomes independent country when French pull out.
1947	British stop refugee ship *Exodus*, send Jewish refugees to Germany.
	United Nations partitions Palestine into Jewish and Arab states.
	Jews proclaim State of Israel; five Arab countries attack.
	United States first to recognize Israel; Soviet Union follows.

1976
Syrian troops enter Lebanon to put down civil war

2003
Parliamentary elections further the gradual reform measures; United States invades Iraq; reform movement in Syria effectively ends

1990
Syria joins U.S.-sponsored coalition to oust Iraq from Kuwait

1976   2007

1982
Suppression of Muslim Brotherhood by Syrian government, especially in Hamah; Israel invades Lebanon to attack PLO bases; clashes with Syrians

2000
Hafez al-Assad dies; son, Bashar, becomes president of Syria. The Damascus Spring, a period of gradual reform, begins

2007
Bashar al-Assad is elected to a second seven-year term as president of Syria

1949	Military overthrows Syrian government; first of many coups.
1957	Crisis in Syrian relations with the West and between Ba'athists and Communists.
1958	Syria joins Egypt in United Arab Republic.
1961	Syria withdraws from United Arab Republic.
1967	Israel defeats Syria, Egypt, and Jordan in Six-Day War; Israel takes Golan Heights from Syria.
1970	Hafez al-Assad becomes president of Syria.
1973	Syria and Egypt attack Israel on Yom Kippur; U.S. Secretary of State Henry Kissinger conducts shuttle diplomacy between Syria and Israel.
1976	Syrian troops enter Lebanon to put down civil war.
1979	Israel and Egypt sign peace treaty.
	United States adds Syria to list of countries that support terrorists.
1982	Suppression of Muslim Brotherhood by Syrian government, especially in Hamah.
	Israel invades Lebanon to attack PLO bases; clashes with Syrians.
	Ronald Reagan sends U.S. Marines into Lebanon to keep order.
1983	Terrorist bomb kills 241 Marines in Beirut.
1984	Marines pull out of Lebanon.
1990	Syria joins U.S.-sponsored coalition to oust Iraq from Kuwait.
2000	Hafez al-Assad dies; son, Bashar, becomes president of Syria.
	"The Damascus Spring," a period of gradual reforms, begins.
2003	Parliamentary elections further the gradual reform measures; United States invades Iraq; reform movement in Syria effectively ends.

2005   Rafiq al-Hariri, a former prime minister of Lebanon who had been critical of Syria's affairs in his country, is assassinated; Syrian intelligence forces are strongly suspected of complicity.

Under intense international pressure, Syria withdraws its military troops from Lebanon, ending nearly three decades of virtual occupation; a UN report indicates that Syrian agents had a hand in the assassination of Hariri.

2006   Protests across the Arab world over the publication of a cartoon considered defamatory toward Islam result in riots that burn the Danish, Norwegian, and French embassies in Damascus; war between Israel and Syria-backed Hezbollah along the Golan border causes more than 1,200 deaths and turns tens of thousands of Lebanese citizens into refugees.

2007   Syria signs major agreements with its largest import partner, China; several anti-Syrian members of Lebanon's parliament and six UN peacekeepers in Lebanon are assassinated, and Syrian agents are accused of complicity; Bashar al-Assad is elected to a second seven-year term as president of Syria.

Bibliography

Commins, David. *Historical Dictionary of Syria*. Lanham, M.D.: Scarecrow Press, 1996.

Congressional Quarterly. *The Middle East*. Washington, D.C.: Congressional Quarterly, 1991.

Dayan, Moshe. *Story of My Life*. New York: William Morrow & Co., 1976.

Elon, Amos. *The Israelis: Fathers and Sons*. New York: Holt, Rinehart & Winston, 1971.

Eytan, Walter. *The First Ten Years: A Diplomatic History of Israel*. New York: Simon & Schuster, 1958.

Gilbert, Martin. *Churchill*. New York: Henry Holt & Co., 1991.

Ginat, Rami, *Syria and the Doctrine of Arab Neutralism*. Brighton: Sussex Academic Press, 2005.

Goodarzi, Jubin. *Syria and Iran: Diplomatic Alliance and Power Politics in the Middle East*. New York: Tauris Academic Studies, 2008.

Graves, Robert. *Lawrence and the Arabian Adventure*. New York: Doubleday, Doran & Co., 1928.

Lawrence, T.E. *Seven Pillars of Wisdom*. New York: Doubleday, Doran & Co., 1935.

Lesch, David. *The New Lion of Damascus: Bashar al-Asad and Modern Syria*. New Haven, Conn.: Yale University Press, 2005.

———. *Syria and the United States: Eisenhower's Cold War in the Middle East*. Boulder, Colo.: Westview, 1992.

Leverett, Flynt. *Inheriting Syria: Bashar's Trial by Fire*. Washington, D.C.: Brookings Institution Press, 2005.

Ma'oz, Moshe. *Modern Syria: From Ottoman Rule to Pivotal Role in the Middle East*. Eastbourne, England: Sussex Academic Press, 1999.

———. *Asad: The Sphinx of Damascus*. New York: Grove/Atlantic, 1990.

Moubayed, Sami. *Damascus Between Democracy and Dictatorship*. Lanham, M.D.: University Press of America, 2000.

O'Brien, Conor Cruise. *The Siege: The Saga of Israel and Zionism.* New York: Simon & Schuster, 1986.

Rabinovich, Itamar. *The Brink of Peace.* Princeton, N.J.: Princeton University Press, 1999.

Shimoni, Yaacov, and Evyatar Levine. *Political Dictionary of the Middle East in the 20th Century.* New York: Quadrangle/The New York Times Book Co., 1974.

Shlaim, Avi. *War and Peace in the Middle East: A Concise History.* New York: Penguin Books, 1995.

Stewart, Desmond. *The Middle East: Temple of Janus.* New York: Doubleday & Co., 1971.

Thubron, Colin. *Mirror to Damascus.* New York: Little Brown & Co., 1967.

Zisser, Eyal. *Asad's Legacy: Syria in Transition.* New York: NYU Press, 2001.

Web Sites

SyriaComment.com

http://www.joshualandis.com/blog/

An influential site maintained by Joshua Landis, a Syria expert at the University of Oklahoma. Contains a current blog, links to current news articles, and much more.

SyrianHistory.com

http://www.syrianhistory.com/

An "online museum" of Syrian history maintained by Syrian political analyst Sami Moubayed.

Further Resources

Beaton, Margaret. *Syria*. New York: Children's Press, 1988.

Haag, Michael. *Syria and Lebanon*. Guilford, Conn.: Globe Pequot Press, 2000.

Hopwood, Derek. *Syria, 1945–1986: Politics and Society*. Sydney, Australia: Unwin, 1988.

Humphreys, Andrew, and Damien Simonis. *Lonely Planet: Syria: A Travel Survivor Kit*. New York: Lonely Planet Publications, 1999.

Seale, Patrick. *Assad of Syria: The Struggle for the Middle East*. Berkeley, Calif.: University of California Press, 1990.

Ziser, Eyal. *Assad's Legacy: Syria in Transition*. New York: New York University Press, 2000.

Web Sites

Creative Syria
http://creativesyria.com/
Syrian culture, arts, history, and current affairs.

Damascus Online
http://www.damascus-online.com/
Everything Syrian.

Souria.com
http://www.souria.com/home.asp
Cultural site about Syria.

Syrian Arab News Agency (SANA)
http://www.sana.org
Syrian news agency.

Syria Online
http://www.syriaonline.com/Categories/aboutsy.htm
Search engine for all things related to Syria.

Syria View/About Syria

http://www.syriaview.net/index.php?option=com_content&task=view&id
=24&Itemid=38

All about Syria.

Picture Credits

Index

About the Contributors

Jack Morrison is a longtime Philadelphia newspaperman. He has worked as a reporter, rewriteman, and editor. He has published poetry and short stories and has edited several novels for a Dell Publishing Company subsidiary.

Adam Woog has written many books for adults, young readers, and children. He lives in his hometown, Seattle, Washington, with his wife and daughter. He would like to thank Dr. James Reilly of the University of Toronto and Dr. David Commins of Dickinson College for their generous help in preparing his contribution to this book.

Arthur Goldschmidt Jr. is a retired professor of Middle East History at Penn State University. He has a B.A. in economics from Colby College and his M.A. and Ph.D. degrees from Harvard University in history and Middle Eastern Studies. He is the author of *A Concise History of the Middle East*, which has gone through eight editions, and many books, chapters, and articles about Egypt and other Middle Eastern countries. His most recent publication is *A Brief History of Egypt*, published by Facts On File in 2008. He lives in State College, Pennsylvania, with his wife, Louise. They have two grown sons.